D1142283

THE
FELT
BOOK

For Gavin, Jack, Kate and Thomas

THE FELT BOOK

Easy-to-make projects for all ages

Clare Beaton

C&B

COLLINS & BROWN

First published in Great Britain in 1994 by

Collins & Brown Limited
Letts of London House
Great Eastern Wharf
Parkgate Road
London SW11 4NQ

1 3 5 7 9 8 6 4 2

British Library Cataloguing in Publication Data:

A catalogue record for this book is available from the
British Library

ISBN Hardback: 1 85585 188 1
ISBN Paperback: 1 85585 215 2

Conceived, edited and designed by Collins & Brown Limited

Editor: Catherine Bradley
Art Director: Roger Bristow
Photography Stylist: Ruth Hope
Photography: Geoff Dann
Designed by: Ruth Hope and Nigel Partridge
Cover design: Ruth Hope

Filmset by Bookworm Typesetting, Manchester
Reproduction by Global Colour, Malaysia
Printed and bound in Italy by New Interlitho SpA, Milan

$\mathscr{C}$ONTENTS

$\mathcal{I}$NTRODUCTION

Legend has it that felt was the creation of St Clement, the patron saint of felt-makers, who put wool in his shoes to keep his feet warm and discovered that the application of heat, pressure and moisture formed a new material. This is a good description of how felt is made, but the material predates St Clement and is almost certainly the oldest manufactured fabric known, in existence long before woven cloth. Since time immemorial nomadic tribes across Asia have made clothing, tents and boots from felt.

Today felt remains a very valuable material in industry with hundreds of uses, and craft felt is much used in window displays and in mounting exhibitions. As a craft material it became very popular in the nineteenth century when appliquéd flower and fruit arrangements padded and stitched onto a background formed charming framed pictures. In this century felt has been popular for making gifts and items for the home. More recently there has been an artistic interest in hand-made felt.

Felt is a remarkable material. Made by compression, it has qualities quite unlike woven cloth. It does not fray when it is cut and yet felt is a firm material, easily pierced with a needle. It comes in a dazzling variety of dense, strong colours and is readily available and cheap. It is very easy to use as it can be sewn or glued and self-adhesive felt is also available. Felt is an ideal foil for all manner of decoration – sequins, braids, fancy stitching or beads. Modern felts are made from a mixture of viscose and wool and can be sponged or dry-cleaned.

This book is divided into sections, each with a theme and both written and illustrated instructions to make all the items featured in the photographs. Some of them are easier to make than others, but none of them requires any specialist skill. When you have decided what you would like to make, first turn to the template you need and find out how much felt is required. The shopping list for each item gives a guide. Take care to check whether you need more than one cut-out for any piece.

Felt can be bought in various sizes from markets as well as fabric and craft shops. It is sold either by the yard or metre, in different widths (all

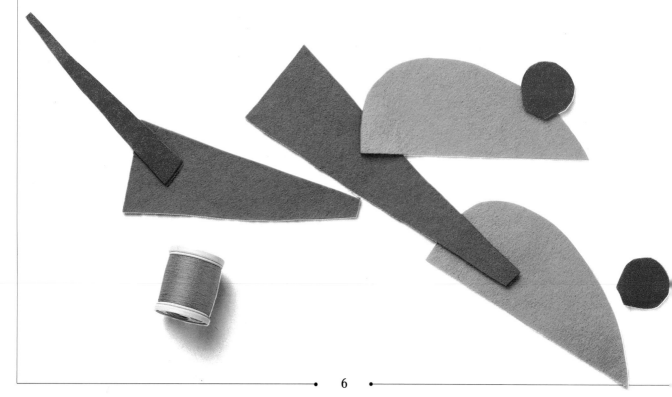

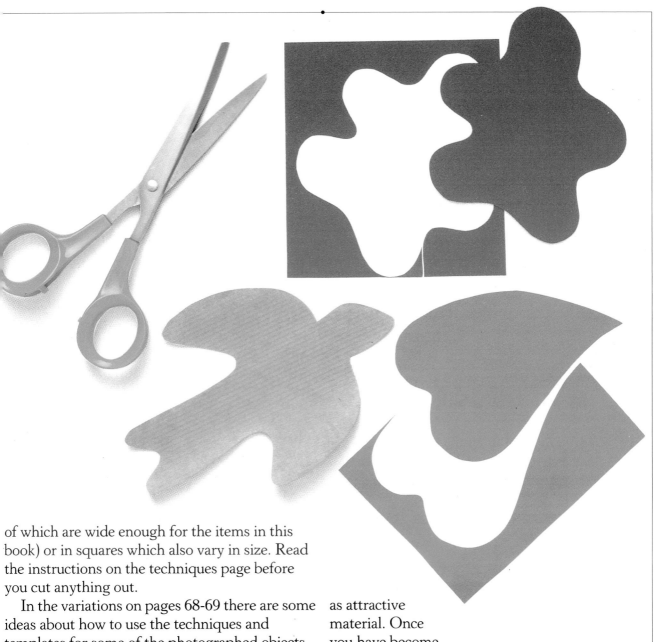

of which are wide enough for the items in this book) or in squares which also vary in size. Read the instructions on the techniques page before you cut anything out.

In the variations on pages 68-69 there are some ideas about how to use the techniques and templates for some of the photographed objects in different ways, varying combinations and colours. Different ways of using the motifs to suit your own particular projects are also featured within the chapters. Felt is a very versatile as well as attractive material. Once you have become familiar with felt, I hope that this book will inspire you to design and make your own creations, choosing from the infinite variety of colours that are now available.

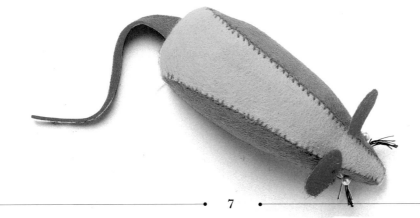

TOOLS AND EQUIPMENT

You do not need any special tools or equipment to work with felt, which is one of the reasons for its increasing popularity. You will probably have everything you need at home already, with the possible exception of a pair of pinking shears, useful for creating the attractive zig-zag edging on some of the projects. Pencils, tracing paper and pins are needed to copy the project templates, which are in the rear section of the book.

Felt provides a marvellous background for all kinds of decorative stitching, sequins, beads, trimmings and so on. Some of the projects in the book use threads of wool to

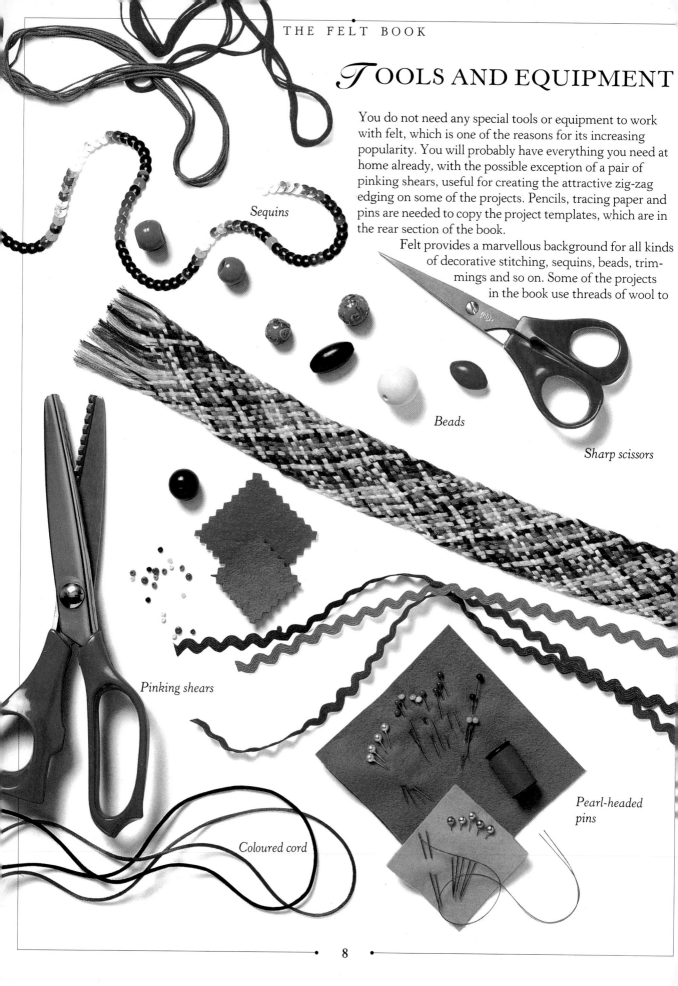

Sequins

Beads

Sharp scissors

Pinking shears

Coloured cord

Pearl-headed pins

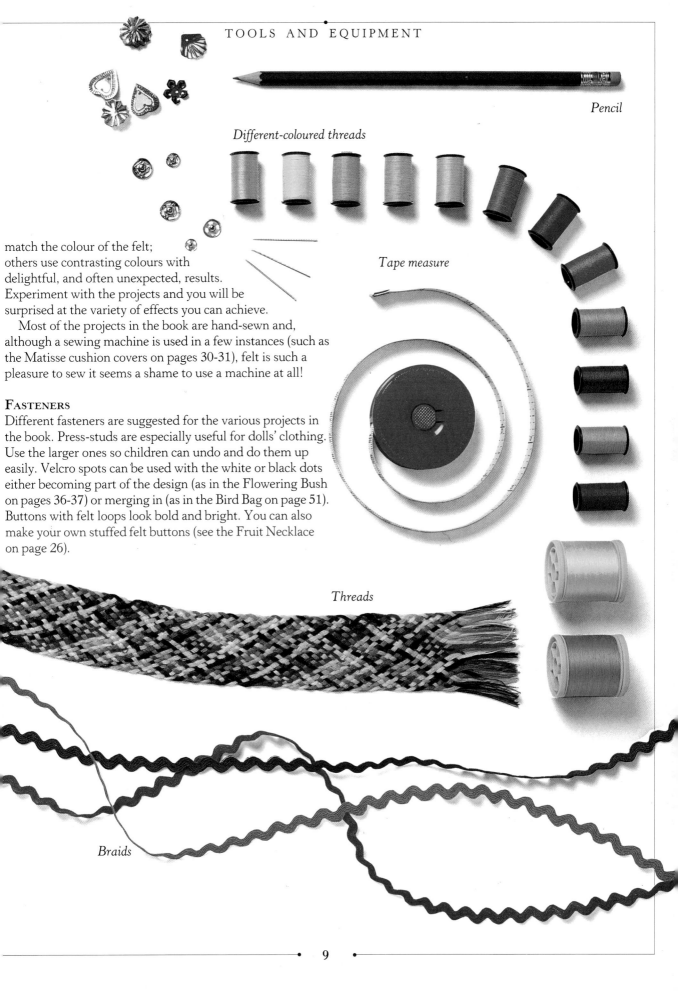

Pencil

Different-coloured threads

Tape measure

match the colour of the felt; others use contrasting colours with delightful, and often unexpected, results. Experiment with the projects and you will be surprised at the variety of effects you can achieve.

Most of the projects in the book are hand-sewn and, although a sewing machine is used in a few instances (such as the Matisse cushion covers on pages 30-31), felt is such a pleasure to sew it seems a shame to use a machine at all!

FASTENERS

Different fasteners are suggested for the various projects in the book. Press-studs are especially useful for dolls' clothing. Use the larger ones so children can undo and do them up easily. Velcro spots can be used with the white or black dots either becoming part of the design (as in the Flowering Bush on pages 36-37) or merging in (as in the Bird Bag on page 51). Buttons with felt loops look bold and bright. You can also make your own stuffed felt buttons (see the Fruit Necklace on page 26).

Threads

Braids

CLOTHES

Felt has always been valued for its durability, warmth and colour. In folk costume it was made into hats and boots and used for its decorative qualities in the making of braces, belts and waistcoats. The items in this chapter follow in that tradition and would make stunning additions to any outfit. The collars can be worn over a wool or velvet dress instead of more conventional lace ones.

CAT COLLAR

· WHAT TO DO ·

1 Pin cats in position evenly around collar, alternating colours, and sew on with small overstitches using matching coloured threads. Add red balls in same way, positioning as shown.

2 Starting from left edge, pin red strip around neck edge on right side with edges matching as shown. Leave 5mm/¼in sticking out beyond left edge of collar.

3 Sew on by machine or hand (in a small running stitch) in red close to edge.

4 Fold the 5mm/¼in end in and pin the red strip over to the back of collar. Sew along edge in small overstitches.

5 When you reach the right hand edge sew the overlapping strip together, also in overstitches.

6 Now make the button loop: fold the strip in two and sew the last 1cm/⅜in under the strip on wrong side of collar. Sew button below strip on front at other end of collar. Press. (You could make your own felt button if you wish, as shown.)

SHOPPING LIST
Felt:
1 × 20cm/8in square of grey
1 × 20cm/8in square of white
Strip of red 37cm/14½in × 2cm/¾in
1 × 32cm/12½in square of navy
Scrap of red
1 navy button
Thread in matching colours

SHAPES TO CUT
See templates 1–3 on page 74.
Cut out collar and appliqué pieces.

Floral Collar

SHAPES TO CUT

See templates 4–12 on page 75.
Cut out collar and appliqué pieces
using pinking shears where
indicated.

SHOPPING LIST
Felt:
1 × 20cm/8in square of purple
1 × 20cm/8in square of yellow
1 × 20cm/8in square of green
1 × 20cm/8in square of pink
1 × 20cm/8in square of blue
Strip of pink 2cm/¾in ×
37cm/14½in, cut one long edge
with pinking shears
Piece of turquoise 40cm/16in ×
30cm/11¾in
1 turquoise button
Yellow 4-ply wool
Thread in matching colours

• WHAT TO DO •

1 Pin green leaves and stalk pieces on front of collar in the 'mirrored' position, as shown. Using small overstitches in matching thread, sew on leaves and stalks – pushing a pink (left) and yellow (right) bud under pinking-sheared edges of the two stalks and also sewing down.

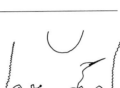

2 Assemble flowers; sew purple petals in position. Place pink (or yellow) crosses on top, then the blue petals and lastly pink (or yellow) pinking-sheared circle. Tack together in centre.

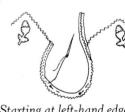

5 Starting at left-hand edge, pin pink strip on to neck edge with the pinking-sheared edge on right side. Overlap left edge by 5mm/¼in and trim off with pinking shears. Starting here, sew through all three layers with small running stitch and matching thread.

3 Place blue circles on top and sew on with seven dots in yellow wool.

4 Sew buds and stalks in position on back. The pink goes in the left-hand corner, yellow in the right.

6 Now make button loop: fold pinking-sheared edge of left-over strip under (forming a roll) and sew together with overstitch. Fold roll in two and sew end securely 1cm/⅜in under strip on the wrong side of collar. Lastly sew button below strip on opposite edge of collar.

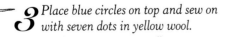

BIRD HAT

SHOPPING LIST

Felt:
25cm/10in of blue
1 × 20cm/8in square of red
1 × 20cm/8in square of cream

Red double-knitting wool
Black 4-ply wool
6 small black beads
Thread in matching colours

SHAPES TO CUT

See templates 13–16 on page 76.
Cut out a band of blue
20cm/8in × 54cm/21¼in, the
four blue crown pieces and
appliqué pieces.

• WHAT TO DO •

1 *Join the crown pieces together with a lacing of red wool. Place the edges of two pieces together and, starting at the points, sew together as shown. Join all four pieces (forming a 'bowl') in this way.*

2 *Pin band along bottom of 'bowl', starting at one join, and tack together. Fold band in two and pin edge along the line of tacking.*

3 *Sew ends of bands together in the same way as with the crown pieces.*

4 *Overstitch along top and bottom of band with red wool.*

5 *Pin bird bodies on to band evenly spaced in alternate red and cream. Sew on in matching thread. Next add the wings and beaks – red ones on cream, cream on red.*

6 *Lastly sew beads on for eyes. Sew legs and feet on with black wool using three stitches for each.*

ƒLIPPERS

SHOPPING LIST
Felt:
25cm/10in of green
1 × 20cm/8in square of blue
1 × 20cm/8in square of
thick red
Red 4-ply wool
Yellow 4-ply wool
Strong green thread (machine)

SHAPES TO CUT

See templates 32–35 on pages 80–81.
This size will fit a size 4 foot.
You can make different sizes by
drawing around the foot on
paper and lengthening or
shortening upper pieces to fit.
Cut out all pieces and divide
into the two slippers.

• WHAT TO DO •

1 Pin two
green pieces
together and sew backs
together in green
thread. Overstitch in
yellow wool all
round top edge.

2 Pin blue toe piece in position,
matching curved edges. Sew on
to slipper in yellow overstitch.

3 Overstitch in yellow
all around bottom
edge, sewing through
all pieces of felt.

4 Next pin blue back
piece in position – fold in
two and fold around back
seam, matching points
at top. Sew on to slipper
and join points together
in yellow overstitch.

5 Embroider yellow and red
stars on the front of slipper,
making sure not to go through to
the 'inside'.

6 Make pompom in red wool with a
3.5cm/1⅜in diameter circle and sew
on to blue toe piece.

7 Pin upper on to sole and
sew two rows of machine
stitching in green thread close
to edges. You can do this by
hand, but machine stitching will be
stronger. Make second slipper in same way.

MITTENS

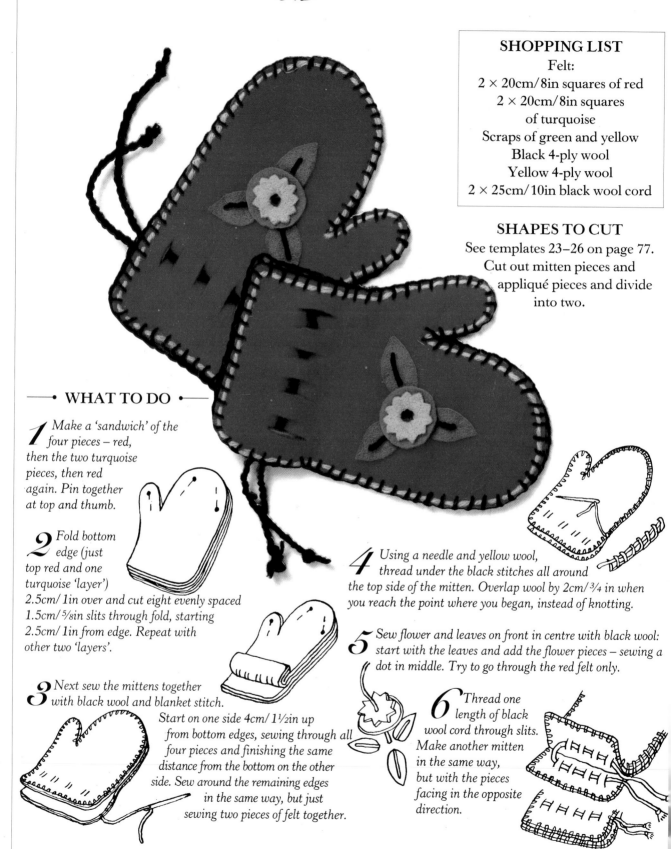

SHOPPING LIST
Felt:
2 × 20cm/ 8in squares of red
2 × 20cm/ 8in squares
of turquoise
Scraps of green and yellow
Black 4-ply wool
Yellow 4-ply wool
2 × 25cm/ 10in black wool cord

SHAPES TO CUT

See templates 23–26 on page 77.
Cut out mitten pieces and
appliqué pieces and divide
into two.

• WHAT TO DO •

1 Make a 'sandwich' of the
four pieces – red,
then the two turquoise
pieces, then red
again. Pin together
at top and thumb.

2 Fold bottom
edge (just
top red and one
turquoise 'layer')
2.5cm/ 1in over and cut eight evenly spaced
1.5cm/ ⅝in slits through fold, starting
2.5cm/ 1in from edge. Repeat with
other two 'layers'.

3 Next sew the mittens together
with black wool and blanket stitch.
Start on one side 4cm/ 1½in up
from bottom edges, sewing through all
four pieces and finishing the same
distance from the bottom on the other
side. Sew around the remaining edges
in the same way, but just
sewing two pieces of felt together.

4 Using a needle and yellow wool,
thread under the black stitches all around
the top side of the mitten. Overlap wool by 2cm/ ¾ in when
you reach the point where you began, instead of knotting.

5 Sew flower and leaves on front in centre with black wool:
start with the leaves and add the flower pieces – sewing a
dot in middle. Try to go through the red felt only.

6 Thread one
length of black
wool cord through slits.
Make another mitten
in the same way,
but with the pieces
facing in the opposite
direction.

Baby's Slippers

Note: *These slippers are most suitable for young babies. For crawling and toddling children, use thick red felt for the soles and enlarge the templates.*

SHAPES TO CUT

See templates 17–22 on pages 76–77. Cut out all the slipper and appliqué pieces and divide into two.

• WHAT TO DO •

1 Sew flower and leaves on front of red upper: first sew on two leaves with large stitch of black wool. Then add turquoise and yellow discs and attach with a dot of wool in the centre.

2 Pin red and turquoise uppers together and sew around all edges with black wool blanket stitch.

3 Join the red and turquoise soles together with black wool blanket stitch.

4 Join back seam of uppers with black overstitch and then pin and join sole to upper, keeping turquoise inside, in same way.

5 With needle and yellow wool, thread under the black stitches around top edges of the upper. Overlap wool by 2cm/¾ in when you reach where you began, instead of knotting.

6 Cut a strip 1cm/⅜in wide and 30cm/11¾in long in red felt. Cut a 1cm/⅜in slit either side of slipper upper where shown and thread strip through. Tie in bow.

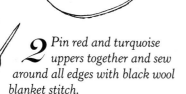

Make the other slipper in the same way.

WAISTCOAT

SHOPPING LIST
Felt:
1 metre/1 yard of red
1 metre/1 yard of black
1 × 20cm/8in square of cream
Black 4-ply wool
Cream and black
thread

SHAPES TO CUT
See templates 27–31 on pages 77–79.
Cut out the waistcoat and
appliqué pieces.

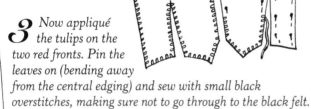

• WHAT TO DO •

1 Pin the two back pieces together and, using wool, blanket stitch together with 1cm/ ³⁄₈in stitches all the way round (including dart edges). Trim with scissors if the pieces do not match exactly. Use as long a piece of wool as possible to avoid too many joins.

2 Join the two front pieces in the same way – making sure you have a left-hand and a right-hand side.

3 Now appliqué the tulips on the two red fronts. Pin the leaves on (bending away from the central edging) and sew with small black overstitches, making sure not to go through to the black felt.

4 Pin the cream flowers on and sew on in cream overstitches. Add the lines, as shown, with black wool and large stitches – about seven on each flower, and three smaller ones on either side of the top of the stalk.

5 Join up the darts with black wool by overstitching between the blanket stitching (fold the black sides together and sew along edge). Add two to three 1cm/ ³⁄₈in stitches at top of dart to finish off.

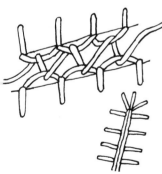

6 Lastly join the fronts to the back in the same way as the darts – along the shoulders and the sides.

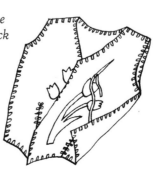

As an attractive alternative, use red tulip shapes on a cream waistcoat background.

JEWELLERY

From the 1920s to the 1940s, felt jewellery was very popular. Flowers, in particular, were made into a great variety of items, including necklaces, brooches and posies to be worn on lapels or hats. A more ethnic influence inspired the Fruit Necklace and Animal Brooches on pages 26 and 27. From the pieces described you can go on to create your own ideas using small scraps of felt left over from the larger projects.

FLORAL NECKLACE

• WHAT TO DO •

1 *Roll each of the two strips of black felt into three and sew together along edge with tiny neat overstitches in black.*

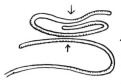

2 *Fold the shorter strip into a 'bow' shape with two loops and long end, as shown. With black thread tack in centre, 9cm/3½in from one end of longer strip – keeping it all together.*

3 *Wrap a small rectangle of black felt around tacking and secure ends on side (with end of long strip pointing left under bow). Sew securely with a few stitches through to cord (to prevent slipping). Sew bottom of press-stud to left of this 'knot'. Sew other half of press-stud on to other end of long strip.*

4 *Turn strips over and sew moon-shaped piece on to centre of strip with small overstitches in black.*

SHOPPING LIST
Felt:
Strip of black 52cm/20½in × 2cm/¾in
Strip of black 42cm/16½in × 2cm/¾in
1 × 20cm/8in square of black
Scraps of pink, yellow, orange, purple, mauve, turquoise and green
Press-stud
Black and coloured threads to match

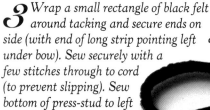

SHAPES TO CUT
See templates 36–40 on page 82. Cut out strips, moon-shaped black backing, leaves (about 18), and flowers (about 37 of varying shapes and sizes including some cut with pinking shears), plus tiny circles for flower centres.

5 *Using green thread double-sew veins on to leaves.*

6 *Starting from the left (with press-stud underneath) begin to sew the flowers and leaves on to moon-shaped backing, using matching or contrasting threads. Sew the centres on as you go and overlap until the black backing is completely covered. Add more flowers if necessary.*

*E*AR-RINGS

*H*AIRSLIDES

SHOPPING LIST
Felt:
Scraps of different-
coloured felt
2 ear-clips
Coloured threads

SHAPES TO CUT
See templates 37–40 on
page 82.
Cut out a set of flowers and
leaves for each ear-ring –
two leaves and seven flowers
for each. Also two
black ovals.

SHOPPING LIST
Felt:
Scraps of different-
coloured felt
2 metal slides
Coloured threads
Fabric glue

SHAPES TO CUT
See templates 37–40 on page 82.
Cut out five flowers and two leaves
for each side – these can all
be different.

• WHAT TO DO •

1 Sew veins on to leaves with double
green thread.

2 Sew centres on to flowers in
a variety of different ways
with different-coloured threads.

3 Sew leaves and flowers on to
both black ovals in identical
positions, overlapping them. Sew clips on
o back of ovals.

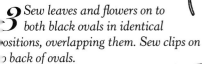

• WHAT TO DO •

1 Sew veins on to leaves with double
green thread. Sew centres on to
flowers in a variety of different ways
with different-coloured threads.

2 Glue on to slides overlapping, and
completely covering, each of the sides.

BUNCH OF FLOWERS

SHOPPING LIST
Felt:
1 × 20cm/8in square of cream
1 × 20cm/8in square of
pale pink
1 × 20cm/8in square of
flesh colour
1 × 20cm/8in square of green
1 × 20cm/8in square of brown
Safety-pin
Fabric glue
Thread in matching colours

SHAPES TO CUT
See templates 41–48 on page 82.
Cut out all pieces and divide petals
and fringed strips into two flowers.

*3 Pin the cream petals around
circle with seams at back and
sew on. Add the flesh-coloured ones
next. Finally sew on the three
single flesh-coloured petals,
alternating between the last six.*

*4 Make the four stalks by
folding the brown strips into
three lengthways and
overstitching in small stitches in
matching thread. Sew three leaves
on to the top of two stalks.*

• WHAT TO DO •

*1 Sew seams down the centre
of all the petals and leaves:
fold each petal or leaf in half
and, starting at the straighter,
bottom end of petals and either end
of leaves, neatly overstitch in
matching thread along fold, finishing
5mm/¼in from end.*

*2 Then make the flowers. The centre
is made by rolling the fringed strips
around one another to form a textured but
flat circle. Start with cream, then the pale
pink, finishing with the flesh-coloured felt,
tacking together on the back as you go.*

*5 Now assemble everything
into a bunch: tack flower
heads together on the back. Turn over
and tack one leaved stalk amongst the
petals of the left-hand flower. Turn once again
and sew two stalks on to the centre of flowers
keeping the ends even with the leaved one. Sew
the other leaved one, bending left.*

*6 Cut an oval in flesh-coloured
felt large enough to cover the
flower backs (not petals). Glue in
position and sew on pin when dry.*

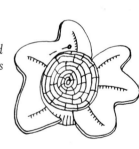

Swallow Hairband

SHOPPING LIST

Felt:

1 × 20cm/8in square of
dark green

1 × 20cm/8in square
of turquoise

1 × 20cm/8in square of yellow

1 × 20cm/8in square of white

Scrap of yellow

2 small black beads

Plastic hairband (about
2.5cm/1in wide)

Toy stuffing

Fabric glue

Thread in matching colours

• WHAT TO DO •

1 First cover the hairband in dark
green felt. Do this in two
halves (the join won't
show). Cut the felt 5mm/
¼in wider than the
hairband on both sides and
glue on to top of band, folding the
ends in underneath and gluing down.
Cut a piece of dark green felt (in two
halves again) a little smaller than
the band and glue on to underside,
covering the ends of the top pieces.

2 Pin and sew two swallow pieces
together with small, neat
overstitches in matching thread, leaving
the head open. Push stuffing in
opening and gently push down into
points. When softly firm, join up opening.

3 Fold beak in two and sew in
yellow thread along fold to attach
it underneath the swallow's head. Sew
on the beads to make eyes on the top of
the head.

SHAPES TO CUT

See templates 49–53 on page 83.
Cut out flowers, leaves and
swallow pieces.

4 Cut the white pinking-
sheared circles between
every other v, making 5mm/
¼in long slits. Place small bits
of stuffing in centre of yellow
circles and draw felt around them
with yellow thread, forming small balls.

5 Next place balls on to white petal
circles, turn over and tack, in white,
attaching them together.

6 In green thread
tack the swallow slightly to the left
of the centre of the hairband and then
add the flowers and leaves in the same
way (see the main photo).

Fruit Necklace

SHOPPING LIST
Felt:
Strip of black 60cm/23½in ×
3.5cm/1⅜in
Scraps of red, pink, mustard,
green, yellow, lemon yellow,
black, lime green and orange

Toy stuffing
Thread in matching colours

SHAPES TO CUT

See templates 54–65 on page 83.
Cut out the black strip, all the
fruit pieces and the button.

• WHAT TO DO •

1 To make the roll and
button, roll up and pin
the black strip lengthways.
Overstitch along edge in small neat stitches in
black. Fold one end
over by 4.5cm/1¾in and
secure (forming a loop). Place
small bit of stuffing on to centre
of red circle. Draw edges of felt
together with red stitching,
forming a small ball. Sew on
to other end of strip.

2 To make the orange, apple and peach, sew the segments
together with small neat overstitches in matching
threads, leaving one seam
unfinished through which the
stuffing is pushed. Stuff and
close the seam. Add black star to
bottom of orange, and leaf and black
stalk (rolled and sewn) to top of apple.
Sew a few stitches in black at
bottom of apple.

3 Sew and stuff lemon
and banana in same
way, finishing off with a few
stitches in black at bottom of each.

4 Sew mustard
-coloured pear
segments together
and stuff. Add leaf
and black stalk to top
and a few stitches in black at bottom.

5 Sew the strawberry in red in the
same way, adding the green
star at the top. Using double yellow
thread, sew dots on to strawberry.

6 Secure fruit to roll,
starting with the banana
in the centre, with a few
stitches in black. The fruit
should be about 2cm/¾in
apart.

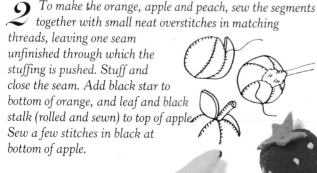

ANIMAL BROOCHES

SHOPPING LIST:

Leopard

Felt:

1 × 20cm/8in square of yellow

Scrap of green

Small black beads

Toy stuffing

Yellow, green and

black thread

Safety-pin

SHOPPING LIST:

Zebra

Felt:

1 × 20cm/8in square of white

Scraps of black and orange

Small blue beads

Toy stuffing

Fabric glue

White, orange and

blue thread

Safety-pin

SHAPES TO CUT

See templates 66–68 on page 84.

Cut out pieces and 6 ×

5mm/¼in wide strips in black.

SHAPES TO CUT

See templates 66–68 on page 84.

Cut out all the pieces.

• WHAT TO DO •

1 Pin the two white zebra halves together and sew all round with small neat overstitches in white, leaving the 'feet' open. Push the stuffing through these openings until firm. Sew up.

• WHAT TO DO •

1 Pin the two yellow pieces together and sew all round with small neat overstitches in yellow, leaving the 'feet' open. Push the stuffing through these openings until firm. Sew up.

2 Pin the two orange pieces together and sew together with orange thread in overstitch, leaving a gap at one end through which to push the stuffing. Sew gap up and sew blue beads all over one side in blue thread.

2 Pin the two green pieces together and sew together with green thread in overstitch, leaving a gap at one end through which to push the stuffing. Then sew gap up. Sew black beads all over one side of the leopard in black thread.

3 Now sew the feet of the zebra on to the beaded side of orange piece. Hold a black stripe against back leg of zebra and trim to fit. Glue in position and repeat with five more stripes. When dry sew a safety-pin on to the centre of the back.

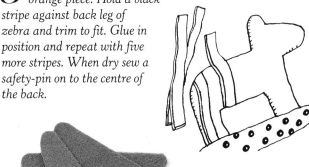

3 Sew 'feet' on to the green piece. Finish by sewing a safety-pin on to the centre of the back.

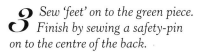

FOR THE HOME

Feltwork pictures were one of the most popular amateur handicrafts of the Regency period. Pieces of felt were stitched on to a background and padded to create a three-dimensional image. By using a variety of cut-outs, padded and unpadded, quite life-like results were achieved. In contrast the cushion covers on pages 30-31 were inspired by the paper cut-out assemblies of Henri Matisse. Just like paper, felt can be glued, so you don't have to sew these if you prefer not to.

MATISSE CUT-OUT CUSHIONS

During the last twenty years of his life, Henri Matisse gave up painting pictures for making assemblies of paper cut-outs. Using a pair of scissors to cut heavy paper painted with gouache, he found a spontaneity equal to that of drawing or painting. By varying or 'flipping' the templates, you can create your own imaginative designs. You can also invent your own shapes and then cut them freehand.

SHOPPING LIST
Flower cushion
Felt:
½ metre/½ yard of blue
½ metre/½ yard of black
1 × 20cm/8in square of wine colour
1 × 20cm/8in square of grey
1 × 20cm/8in square of white

SHAPES TO CUT
See templates 79–84 on pages 86–87. Cut out all pieces including a 30.5cm/12in square of blue felt and a strip of black felt, 2.5cm/1in wide × 122cm/48in long.

• WHAT TO DO •

1 Arrange the pieces, including the strips, into desired configuration on the blue felt.

2 Pick them up one at a time (starting with the strips) and position with fabric glue. Apply glue to one side of the shape only and press down firmly. Shapes can be sewn in position if preferred.

The line illustrations show some of the attractive and varied designs that can be made using these basic shapes.

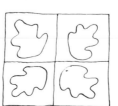
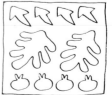

SHOPPING LIST
Leaf cushion
Felt:
½ metre/½ yard of black
¼ metre/¼ yard of white
¼ metre/¼ yard of grey
1 × 20cm/8in square of
wine colour
Fabric glue

SHAPES TO CUT
See templates 79–84 on pages 86–87.
Cut out all pieces including two
strips, one white and one grey,
measuring about 30.5cm/12in ×
6.5cm/2½in. Also cut out a
30.5cm/12in square of black felt.

• WHAT TO DO •

*1 Arrange the pieces, including the strips, into the
final design on the black felt. Use fabric
glue to fix the pieces in position.*

SHOPPING LIST
White bird cushion
Felt:
½ metre/½ yard of grey
½ metre/½ yard of black
1 × 20cm/8in square of pink
1 × 20cm/8in square of
wine colour
1 × 20cm/8in square of brown
1 × 20cm/8in square of white
Thread in contrasting colours

SHAPES TO CUT
See templates 79–84 on pages 86–87.
Cut out all pieces including a
30.5cm/12in square of grey.

• WHAT TO DO •

*1 Pin cut-outs on to the square of grey
felt and sew on with a neat small
running stitch in contrasting threads.*

*To make up the cushions you will need a
50cm/19½in square of black felt, some
black thread and a 30cm/11¾in square
cushion pad. Press the felt and machine
stitch to produce a 30.5 cm/12in square
of black to make the cushion back. Sew
the back and front together, right sides
together, and leave one side open. Insert
cushion pad and sew up.*

Teddy Nursery Frieze

SHOPPING LIST
Felt:
20cm/8in of cream
1 × 20cm/8in square of
donkey brown
1 × 20cm/8in square of
dark beige
1 × 20cm/8in square of ginger
1 × 20cm/8in square of orange
1 × 20cm/8in square of mauve
1 × 20cm/8in square of yellow
Scraps of blue, turquoise and
dark turquoise

Red 4-ply wool
Thin card
Thread in black, cream and
colours to match balloons

SHAPES TO CUT
See templates 69–72 on page 84.
Cut out the nine teddies and
fourteen balloons. Cut out the
background piece in cream – a
rectangle 94cm/37in ×
30cm/11¾in. Cut the
card template.

• WHAT TO DO •

1 Mark out a scallop edge with the card
template, placing the curve on the long edge
of cream felt. Start with half the curve, marking
around the template with a soft pencil and continue
with the complete curve until the other end. Finish with
a second half curve. Cut out carefully with scissors.

2 Turn the cream felt over and
pin the first teddy in position,
starting with a donkey
brown one. It should
be 5cm/2in in from the left-hand edge and 7.5cm/3in up from
the 'bottom' of the first full curve. Sew all around edge with
tiny neat overstitching in cream thread.

3 Repeat with all eight remaining
teddies. They should almost be
holding hands in most cases and actually
holding hands once or twice – just check
that the last one will be the same distance
from the edge as the first. They should be
slightly leaning this way and that, with
none of the same colour next to one another.

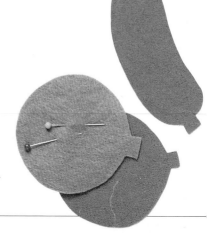

Felt colours of teddies in main picture – left to right:
Donkey Brown · Dark Beige · Donkey Brown · Ginger · Dark Beige
Ginger · Dark Brown · Dark Beige · Ginger

Felt colours of balloons – left to right: Orange · Yellow
Mauve · Yellow (long) · Blue · Turquoise · Dark Turquoise · Yellow
(long) · Orange · Mauve · Blue (long) · Orange · Turquoise · Mauve

4 Sew on the faces in black thread used double; a few stitches for the dot eyes and noses and single stitches for the mouth.

5 The balloons are sewn on with overstitch and thread of matching colour. Pin in position one or two at a time. Where one overlaps another there is no need to sew the edge that is covered.

6 Now sew the strings of the balloons with double black thread and a small continuous running stitch. Start the sewing on the top of the teddies' paws and finish with one or two stitches across the balloon openings. Gently mark the line with a soft pencil first to ensure a straight line.

7 Finish the frieze with blanket stitching all around the edge in red wool.

8 The frieze can be pinned along the edge of a window-sill or frame or attached by red ribbon ties to the side of a cot. If you have a particular place in mind and the length needs altering, either extend the length and number of teddies or reduce the length to fit.

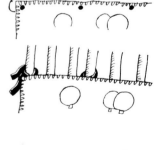

TULIP BASKET PICTURE

SHAPES TO CUT
See templates 73–78 on page 85.
Cut out all the basket, tulip, leaf
and stalk pieces. Also cut a 30.5cm/
12in square from the black felt.

• WHAT TO DO •

SHOPPING LIST

Felt:
½ metre/ ½ yard of black
1 × 20cm/ 8in square of brown
1 × 20cm/ 8in square of green
Scraps of red, pink, orange,
yellow and cream
Red 4-ply wool
Pink 4-ply wool
Orange 4-ply wool
Yellow 4-ply wool
Toy stuffing
Green thread

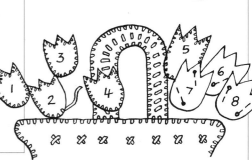

1 Start with the basket: pin bottom part in position centred and 6cm/ 2¼in up from bottom of black felt square. Sew all around edge with neat overstitches in pink wool, allowing a little looseness in the felt to be taken up by the stuffing. Leave a small opening to push this through and distribute evenly to give a gentle padding. Sew hole up. Stitch rows of small pink crosses across basket. All the stitching and knots can appear on the back as it will never be shown.

2 Add the brown handle centred on top of the basket – this isn't padded. Sew all round as before and then add some decorative pink stitches around the handle.

3 Sew the tulips on in two 'groups' in the order given. Use neat overstitching in matching wool – gently padding with stuffing before completing the whole shape. The orange tulip in the left group has a leaf underneath it, therefore leave the right-hand side open until later.

4 Next add the leaves. These are sometimes folded and only partially sewn on to create a relief effect. Sew three in position on the left side with green thread. The centre one should be partly under the orange tulip which is sewn down once the leaf is in position. Cut the central leaf down to 2.5cm/ 1in and sew on to top of basket. Add the last three on to the right-hand group of tulips as shown.

5 Make the cream flowers now. Fold the three green stalks each into three and overstitch along fold with small neat stitches in green. Cut the end of the stalks down to 2.5cm/ 1in. Fold fringed circles in two and sew down under the semi-circular tops of stalks.

6 Sew on to picture as shown in the main photo, just stitching along stalk.

FLOWERING BUSH

SHOPPING LIST
Felt:
50cm/19½in of green
1 × 20cm/8in square of yellow
Scraps of black, red, brown,
mauve, turquoise, pink,
white and grey

7 white Velcro spots
(or Velcoins)
2 small red beads
Thin card
Fabric glue
Threads in contrasting colours

SHAPES TO CUT
See templates 88–114 on
pages 88–89.
Cut out the two green
bush pieces, card and a strip of
green 15cm/6in × 1cm/⅜in.
Cut out all the pieces for the
cut-outs separately – the items
are drawn to show how they
should be assembled on the
green backing felt. Also, cut
out the dots of Velcro if not
using Velcoins.

Bee
Stitch yellow piece on to black body with small black overstitches along straight edges. Sew six stitches in purple on inside edge of wings. Stick on green felt backing.

• WHAT TO DO •

1 Glue the seven yellow flowers, spacing them evenly, on one green piece. Glue one side of the dots of white Velcro in centre of each. Using light green thread used double, sew large stitches all over green felt.

Snail
Sew spiral in white on grey piece. Attach to body piece and stick on to backing.

2 Apply glue to one side of card and stick back of floral bush piece firmly on to it. Glue the strip of green felt in a loop at centre top of card. Glue second piece of green felt on to this side of card. Glue scalloped edges together, and press firmly.

Bird
Make two birds facing different ways: one with a mauve body and turquoise wings and the other with a turquoise body and mauve wings. Using pale pink thread, stitch over wings and breasts of birds. Sew bead on to centre of white eye and sew in position. Assemble (with beaks) and stick on to backing.

3 Next make the cut-outs. All sewing is done with thread used double. After all the pieces have been cut and stitched together, glue them in position on to green felt. Cut the green felt around edges of pieces when dry to form a backing. Glue the other side of circles of Velcro on to centre of the back of each cut-out. See steps **a–e** below.

Butterfly
Sew yellow spots on to wings with mauve thread, sew stars and mauve spots on with white thread dots. Sew seven mauve stitches along inside edge of wings. Assemble (with brown body) and stick on to backing.

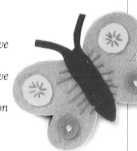

a

b

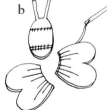

Caterpillar
Sew around edge with yellow stitches and add a row of stitches down centre. Sew white eyes in position with black dot. Glue on to backing and cut with matching pinking shear cuts.

c

d

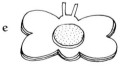

Ladybird
Glue black spots on to red body. Sew white eyes in position on head with black dot. Assemble (with legs) and stick on to backing.

e

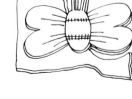

4 Finally, stick cut-outs on to flowers in the bush, using the Velcro.

TOYS

The bright colours and soft feel of felt make it particularly suitable for toy-making and decorating a child's room. The mobiles make a bright addition to a baby's room whilst older children will enjoy making the Finger Puppets (pages 42-43). These are easily adapted to create their own favourite animals.

$\mathcal{B}$IRD $\mathcal{M}$OBILE

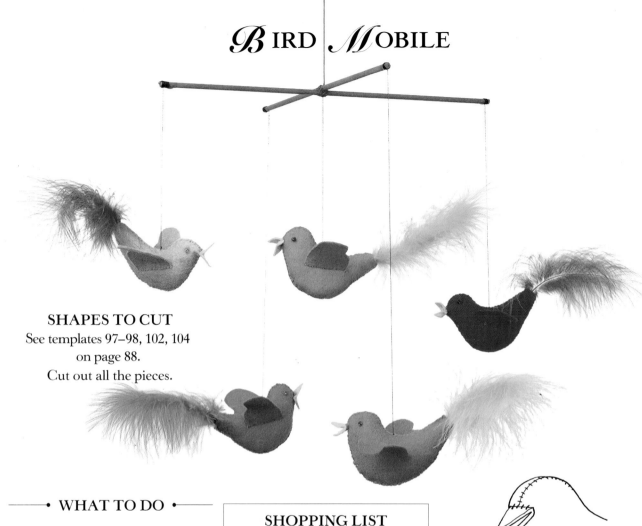

SHAPES TO CUT
See templates 97–98, 102, 104
on page 88.
Cut out all the pieces.

• WHAT TO DO •

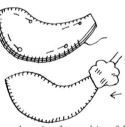

1 Pin each pair of matching felt
halves together and sew around edge
with small neat overstitching in
matching thread. Leave the tail end open
and push in stuffing until softly rounded.

2 Pin wings in position on either side
pointing upwards and sew on to
body along edge in neat stitches of
matching thread.

SHOPPING LIST
Felt:
1 × 20cm/8in square of red
1 × 20cm/8in square
of turquoise
1 × 20cm/8in square of mauve
1 × 20cm/8in square of orange
1 × 20cm/8in square of green
Scrap of yellow
10 small glass coloured beads
1 fluffy feather to match each
felt colour
Toy stuffing
Thread in matching colours

3 Fold beak pieces in half and sew in
yellow thread along fold to attach
just below curve of head.

4 Sew beads on for eyes and push end
of feather firmly into tail opening.

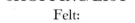

Butterfly Mobile

SHOPPING LIST

Felt:

2 × 20cm/8in squares of
dark brown

1 × 20cm/8in square of cream

1 × 20cm/8in square of
flesh colour

1 × 20cm/8in square of
pale green

1 × 20cm/8in square of
pale pink

1 × 20cm/8in square of
pale blue

Scraps of mustard, grey,
mauve, orange and pink

Fabric glue

Thread in matching and
contrasting colours

SHAPES TO CUT

See templates 85–87 on page 88.
Cut out all the pieces.

• WHAT TO DO •

1 Glue two pairs of coloured spots on to one side of each pair of wings using matching colours, but in random order – mauve and mustard on pale green; mauve and grey on cream; orange and grey on pale pink; pink and orange on pale blue and finally mustard and pink on flesh-coloured felt.

2 Roll up the dark brown body pieces from edge furthest from antennae, pin and oversew together along edge with overstitches in matching thread.

3 Oversew around coloured spots, on one side only, with contrasting thread used double. Sew six stars, as shown, in contrasting thread on same side.

4 Glue two pairs of spots on to cover other side of wings, stitching from the other side.

5 Fold wings in two with the glued spots inside, and blanket stitch around edge of wings with contrasting coloured thread used double. Sew the two wings together on both sides 2cm/¾in up from fold.

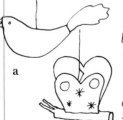

6 Pin wings on to body 1cm/⅜in up from antennae. Sew wings on along fold with small overstitches in brown thread, sewing along both sides of wings.

• WHAT TO DO •

SHOPPING LIST:

To make up the mobiles

1 × 122cm/4ft length of thin
wooden dowelling

Red or mustard paint

Double-sided tape

Invisible thread

1 Cut dowelling into four equal lengths of 30.5cm/12in and paint two in red (for the birds) or two in mustard (for the butterflies). Leave to dry.

2 Cut thread into five varying lengths – from 38cm/15in to 48cm/19in long. Using a needle, knot one end on to centre of bird's back and with the butterfly mobile knot one end 1cm/⅜in down in the centre of the inside of butterfly wings, tying them loosely together (see **a**).

3 Cross two painted dowels together at their half-way point and (you will need another pair of hands here!) secure together with small strips of double-sided tape (removing backing). Wind round the end of a long length of thread to give the desired drop from the ceiling. The dowels should form a cross (see **b**).

4 Wind a narrow strip of double-sided tape round the end of each stick and wind round the end of thread with bird or butterfly attached until secure. Add the longest threaded object to centre in the same way (see **c**).

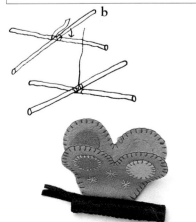
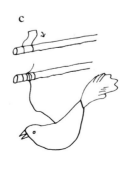

FARM FINGER PUPPETS

• WHAT TO DO •

Cow

1 *Pin black body pieces together and sew around edge (leaving bottom open) with small black overstitching. Pin and sew on the two white patches using white thread.*

2 *Fold ears in two at blunt end and sew on at either side of the back of head attaching the horns just in front.*

3 *Sew pink nose in position with pink thread, nose holes in black. Sew yellow beads for eyes with yellow thread.*

4 *Fold tail into a roll and sew with black overstitches leaving fringed end free. Sew other end half-way up the back of body.*

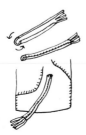

SHAPES TO CUT
See templates 119–137 on page 91. Cut out all the pieces. The body shape is the same for all the animals.

Pig

1 *Pin pink body pieces together and sew around edge (leaving bottom open) with pink overstitching. Sew on ears in pink, folding them down along seam at top of head.*

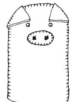

2 *Sew red bead eyes just under ear points. Sew grey nose in position and sew nose holes in black.*

3 *Roll tail and sew together with pink overstitching. Knot once and sew on to the body, 2cm/¾in up from bottom on the back.*

Sheep

1 Pin white body pieces together and sew around edge with white overstitching in the 'v's of the pinking-sheared cuts. Leave the bottom open.

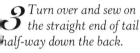

2 Pinch ears together at blunt end and sew ends on to either side of the front of the head in white. Sew turquoise beads on for eyes. Using black thread double-sew a nose and mouth on to the head.

3 Turn over and sew on the straight end of tail half-way down the back.

Horse

1 Pin brown body pieces together and sew around edge (leaving bottom open) with brown overstitching. Fold bottom corners of ears in and sew on to top of head in brown. Sew nose piece on in grey and blue beads for eyes above nose.

2 Using the black wool double, and starting between the ears at front, push needle through felt, leaving about 1.5cm/⅝in of wool sticking out. Push in and out down the back, stopping half-way down, leaving even loops of wool all the way. Cut last bit of wool 1.5cm/⅝in long. Cut through the loops.

3 Form a tail in same way by making one big loop 6cm/2¼in long and 2cm/¾in up from bottom.

Chicken

1 Pin orange body pieces together and sew around edge (leaving bottom open) with orange overstitching. Using red thread, sew the comb on top of the head along the seam.

2 Sew the yellow beak pieces together around edges and, with yellow thread, sew on to head vertically, 1cm/⅜in from top. Sew blue beads on either side of top of beak for eyes. Add small comb in red under the beak.

3 With orange thread, sew tail vertically on to centre of back, starting from the bottom.

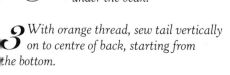

MONSTER GLOVE PUPPET

SHOPPING LIST
Felt:
¼ metre/yard of red
1 × 20cm/8in square of yellow
Scraps or squares of many
colours including black
Fabric glue
Toy stuffing
Yellow and red thread

SHAPES TO CUT
See templates 115–118 on
page 90.
Cut out pieces,
including approximately
100 multi-coloured
strips very roughly
measuring 1.5cm/⅝in
× 7cm/2¾in.

→ WHAT TO DO ←

1 Starting at the bottom
of a red piece, sew by
machine or hand running stitch
a row of strips about 2.5cm/
1in up from the bottom
edge. Continue covering in
strips by adding five further
evenly spaced rows finishing on
top of hands and head. Do the same
to the second red piece.

2 Pin two pairs of horn pieces together
and join each pair with small yellow
overstitching around edges.

3 Pin the red pieces together and sew
along edge with a red running stitch.
At the top of each hand pin and sew in
three claws. Pin and sew in the two
horns on top of the head.

4 Make the eyes by placing a small piece
of stuffing on to the centre of the yellow
circles and drawing the felt around it with
yellow stitches, forming a small firm ball.
Sew these eyes into position below horns.

5 Glue two small black dots on to the
eyes' inner side.

Doll and Her Clothes

Children will love to dress this charming felt doll in her indoor and
outdoor clothes. She is easy to make, and soft enough to be a safe toy
even for very young children. When you have made up the ideas
on the following pages, experiment with different colours
and outfits to provide a wardrobe for all occasions!

SHOPPING LIST
Body
Felt:
30cm/12in or 3 × 20cm/8in
squares of flesh colour
Aubergine-coloured chunky
knit wool
Toy stuffing
Blue, flesh-coloured, brown
and red thread

SHAPES TO CUT
See templates 138–141 on page 92.
Cut out all 12 pieces.

For knickers see page 46

For coat see page 47

For dress see page 47

• WHAT TO DO •

1 Pin all the pair pieces together – the head, body, two arms and two legs. In flesh-coloured thread sew around each in small neat overstitching, leaving an opening for stuffing. Stuff each piece until firm and solid and sew up holes.

2 Using the flesh-coloured thread double, attach head, arms and legs to body. (Sew the seam of the part to be attached to the seam of the body.) The limbs should be securely sewn on, but able to flop.

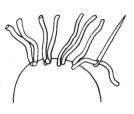

3 Sew face on in coloured threads used double: start with the eyes, making dots in blue; then make the lashes with four single stitches over the eyes. Add the nose with a single stitch (sewn twice) in brown. Sew a curve of red stitches underneath for the mouth.

4 Cut the wool into 25cm/10in lengths. Thread a length at a time on to a large darning needle and, starting at top front just in front of the seam, push needle in and out. Remove needle from wool and pull the two strands of wool to equal lengths. Knot the wool.

5 Repeat all over head, down to just below the eyes and across back of head to the other side – covering the top half of the head. The stitches should be 5mm/¼in apart.

6 When the hair is finished, brush down at the back with your hand and trim ends of wool with scissors to form a longish bob.

• WHAT TO DO •

1 Pin the two pieces together and join with small white over-stitching at side and crotch seams.

2 Cut lengths into two equal lengths. Tack in white along the straight edges of the lace and pull until the lace matches the length around the leg holes. Knot and pin around leg hole and sew over tacking in white running stitches. Repeat for other leg hole.

3 Pull knickers on to doll and sew all around the waist (on to the doll) in small white overstitches.

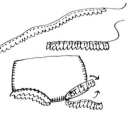

SHOPPING LIST
Knickers
Felt:
1 × 20cm/8in square of white
46cm/18in length of white lace
White thread

SHAPES TO CUT
See template 148 on page 95.
Cut out the two pieces.

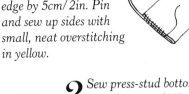

1 Fold bag piece up from straight short edge by 5cm/2in. Pin and sew up sides with small, neat overstitching in yellow.

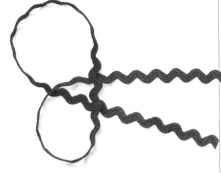

2 Sew press-stud bottom in position 2cm/¾in up from bottom and centred. Sew top of press-stud on to rounded flap 5mm/¼in down from edge and centred.

3 Sew on flowers and leaves on other side of rounded flap: first sew leaves on with central stitching in double yellow thread. Sew flower in centre with yellow stitching.

4 Lastly open the flap and make two small holes 1cm/⅜in in from either side just above the fold. Thread cord in one hole (from outer side) and through the other (to outer side). Pull until ends are even and knot together.

SHOPPING LIST
Bag
Felt:
1 × 20cm/8in square of
deep yellow
Scraps of blue and green
35cm/14in red cord
1 press-stud
Yellow thread

SHAPES TO CUT
See templates 143-145 on page 93.
Cut out bag and appliqué pieces.

SHOPPING LIST
Dress
Felt:
2 × 20cm/8in squares of blue
38cm/15in orange
ric-rac braid
38cm/15in red ric-rac braid
2 press-studs
Blue, orange and red thread

SHAPES TO CUT
See template 142 on page 93.
Cut out pieces.

• WHAT TO DO •

*1 Pin the two pieces together and sew together up the sides in small overstitching in blue (see **a**).*

*2 Sew the press-studs on to the straps now: the tops centred at the top of the straps on the underside; and the bottoms on the tops of corresponding straps on the top side (see **b**).*

*3 Pin the orange ric-rac braid around the bottom of the dress about 1cm/⅜in from bottom edge, overlapping the ends. Sew on, by hand or machine, with small stitches in orange. Pin the red braid 1cm/⅜in above this and attach in the same way (see **c**).*

SHOPPING LIST
Coat
Felt:
25cm/10in × 15cm/6in piece
of blue
1 metre/1 yard orange
ric-rac braid
1 metre/1 yard red ric-rac braid
Blue, orange and red thread

SHAPES TO CUT
See templates 146–147 on pages
94–95.
Cut out pieces.

• WHAT TO DO •

*1 Pin the two front pieces to the back piece. Sew along the shoulder, sleeve and sides in small blue overstitching (see **d**).*

*2 Pin the orange ric-rac braid all around neck, sides and back, starting behind at the neck 1cm/⅜in from edge. Overlap by about 1.5cm/⅝in, trimming off remainder. Sew on with small stitches in orange thread, by hand or machine (see **e**).*

*3 Add the red braid in the same way 1cm/⅜in above the orange braid (see **f**).*

GIFTS

In an age of mass-production and commercialization a hand-made
individual gift has a special value. As felt is also an ideal material for
children to use, some of the simpler projects (like the Mouse Pincushion
on page 53) would be an excellent introduction to sewing
and gift-making for them.

FLORAL PURSE

SHOPPING LIST
Felt:
¼ metre/ ¼ yard of black
¼ metre/ ¼ yard of red
Scraps of green, pink
and yellow
1 large press-stud
Red, green and black thread

SHAPES TO CUT
See templates 149–155 on page 95.
Cut out flower pieces, and the red
and black felt in two strips
measuring 33.5cm/ 13¼in ×
15cm/ 6in.

• WHAT TO DO •

1 Cut one end of the black and red felt
pieces into a curve by rounding the
two corners. Then measure 22cm/ 8½in
from the straight end of the black piece
and mark either side with a pin. Cut
between these pins around curve with
pinking shears.

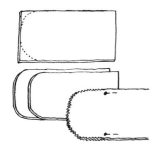

2 Pin the red and black pieces
together and, keeping the red
inside, fold up from the straight edge
by 11cm/ 4¼in. Pin the two sides
together. Overstitch sides together
with red thread used double.

3 Next, using red thread used
double, sew a row of French
knots all around pinking-sheared
edge 5mm/ ¼in from edge. Keep the
underside (on the red felt) neat.

4 Make the flowers next: pinch
bottom of pink petals together
and add two yellow pieces to each flower.
Wrap wide end of stalks around them
and secure tightly with green overstitching
at the back. Continue sewing down to end of stalks.

5 Add leaves to stalks with green
overstitching – one leaf to one
flower and two to the other. Place
close together centred on front of
purse and secure with black stitching
along back of stalks.

6 Lastly sew top of press-stud under
flap and the bottom in corresponding
position below.

BIRD BAG

SHAPES TO CUT
See templates 156–159 on page 96.
Cut out appliqué pieces and put to
one side.

• WHAT TO DO •

1 Cut card into rectangle measuring 46cm/ 18in × 20cm/ 8in and mark off into five different-sized lengths with pencil lines as shown. Fold along each line and bend over.

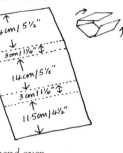

14cm/5½"
3cm/1¼"
14cm/5½"
3cm/1¼"
11.5cm/4½"

2 Open out and place on to black felt and cut around it allowing about 2cm/¾in overlap. Cut corners of felt off and stick felt on to card; fold overlapping pieces over and stick down, pressing firmly. Cut another piece of black felt very slightly smaller than card and stick on the side with the overlapping pieces, covering them.

3 Cut two strips of black felt (for the bag sides) measuring 25cm/ 10in × 5cm/2in and stick down. Fold in half lengthways, making two 12.5cm/5in lengths. Cut the two corners off the unfolded ends with two 1cm/⅜in cuts. Cut double-sided tape into 1cm/⅜in strips and stick around three sides as shown.

4 Fold short section of bag up and hold parallel to back. The side pieces fit in here. Remove backing from tape and stick each side piece on to edge of short section first, then on to the bottom and back of bag. Press firmly together. Overstitch edges of side and main pieces together with black thread used double. Use a thimble.

5 Next make the handle. Cut card into a strip measuring 38cm/15in × 2cm/¾in. Place on to black felt and cut around it allowing 1cm/⅜in overlap. Glue on to felt and fold and glue sides over, but leave ends. Cut another strip of felt very slightly narrower than the handle and the same length (minus the overlaps). Glue down covering overlapped side.

6 Attach to bag by gluing the overlapping ends on to bag sides 4cm/1½in down from the tops of the side. Overstitch with black thread used double around handle ends on to bag sides.

7 Glue appliqué design on to front flap and press. Glue the other half of piece to front of bag. Add Velcro to underside of front flap.

BASKET BOX

SHAPES TO CUT
See template 160 on page 96.
Cut out basket piece.

• WHAT TO DO •

1 Measure the sides and top and bottom of
the box you're covering and cut out felt
accordingly. Cut felt slightly
larger and trim once it's
stuck on, to cover perfectly.

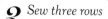

3 Sew three rows
of small crosses in the wool on the basket. Cut
off knot and glue the basket on to top of covered box.
Press down.

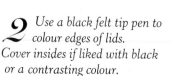

2 Use a black felt tip pen to
colour edges of lids.
Cover insides if liked with black
or a contrasting colour.

4 Measure length of braid
with 1cm/³⁄₈in overlap to fit
around sides of box. Glue around
centre of lid sides.

ℳOUSE 𝒫INCUSHION

SHOPPING LIST
Felt:
1 × 20cm/8in square of
deep yellow
1 × 20cm/8in square
of turquoise
Scrap of bright pink
2 pearl-headed pins
Toy stuffing
Green and black thread

SHAPES TO CUT
See templates 161–162, 165,
166–167 on page 97.
Cut out all the pieces.

• WHAT TO DO •

1 Sew large yellow piece to curved edge
of side piece with small neat overstitching in green,
matching the pointed ends. Add the other side in same way.

2 Add the smaller yellow
piece to make the
bottom, starting at the
pointed nose and leaving the
end open for the stuffing. Push
stuffing in until firm and rounded and
sew up the opening.

3 Pinch smallest ends of
ears together and sew on
body 3cm/1¼in up from nose on
seams, in green.

4 Add tail, sewing wide end to
the centre of the back seam.

5 Using double black
thread push needle
through turquoise felt between
nose and ears, cutting thread on
either side to make whiskers about
2cm/¾in long. Repeat six times.

6 Push pins into mouse
between ears and whiskers
for eyes.

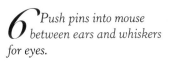

HEART BOOKMARKS

SHAPES TO CUT

See templates 168–169 on page 98. Cut out the three bookmark pieces and the tracing paper rectangle. Trace the heart shapes on to the paper.

SHOPPING LIST
Felt:
1 × 20cm/8in square of navy
1 × 20cm/8in square of red
1 × 20cm/8in square of blue
Fabric glue
White thread

• WHAT TO DO •

Red and navy bookmark (right)

1 Cut the heart shapes out of the red piece: fold the red felt in half lengthways and press to ensure a sharp folded edge. Place the tracing paper template on top, matching the left-hand edge to the fold. Pin and carefully cut out the heart shapes. Unpin tracing paper and open the felt strip. Press flat. Keep the heart pieces to one side.

2 Using white thread double, sew an overstitch around each heart. Be careful not to stretch the heart shapes.

3 Sew small stars between each heart on either side plus one at the bottom. Use white thread double and make four stitches for each.

4 Glue red piece on to navy one and press firmly together.

Red and blue bookmark (left)

1 Decorate each of the four cut-out hearts with double white thread: one with small crosses; one with small spots; another with a small running stitch around the edge; and the last with a criss-cross pattern made from large running stitches.

2 Sew all around the blue strip with an overstitch in double white thread. Remember to keep it neat on both sides.

3 Glue on the red decorated hearts, evenly spaced down one side of strip and centred, in this order from top: crosses, running stitch, criss-cross and spots. Press down in position firmly.

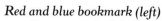

Shell Needlecase

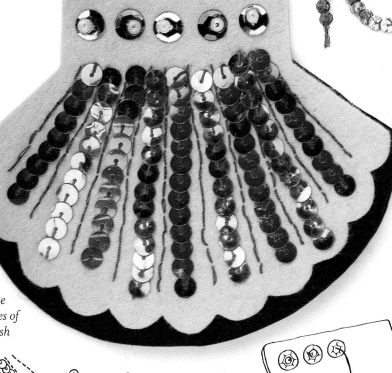

SHOPPING LIST

Felt:
1 × 20cm/8in square of black
1 × 20cm/8in square of
pale pink
5 different-coloured large
faceted sequins
5 small pearl beads
½ metre/½ yard of orange
sequins
½ metre/½ yard of pink
sequins
1 × 20cm/8in square of fine
wool fabric or similar
Fabric glue
Black, purple and pale
pink thread

SHAPES TO CUT

See templates 163–164 on page 97.
Cut out the three shell shapes in
felt. Cut three inside 'leaves' from
fabric wool about 5mm/¼in
smaller all round, and cut the
curves with pinking shears.

• WHAT TO DO •

1 Mark ten points (as shown on template 164) and use as guides for the straight lines of double purple running stitch from the point to the v between the curves of scalloped edging. Start at the point and finish 1cm/³⁄₈in before scalloped edge.

2 Measure the orange and pink sequins into lengths to fit between the purple stitching, starting and ending with pink (five rows) and alternating with the orange (four rows). Pull two sequins off one end of each length and fold under – the other end can be cut just after the last sequin.

3 Glue down between stitching, gluing any threads underneath. Apply the glue in a fine line along back of the sequins and on the felt to run between the stitching lines.

4 With pink thread sew the five large faceted sequins with a pearl bead on top in a row at top of shell.

5 Glue pink sequinned shell to one black shell shape with top and side edges matching.

6 Sew the inner 'leaves' on to other black shape at the top in black thread. Glue along top over stitching and press firmly on to the other black shape to form the needlecase.

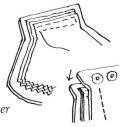

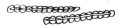

ſPECIAL DAYS

Part of the enjoyment of festive occasions
is the preparation and making of decorations for the home.
The number of attractive Christmas decorations that can be made
from felt is almost infinite. Other special days such as
Valentine's Day or Easter also provide ideal
occasions for felt projects.

EASTER BASKET

SHAPES TO CUT
See templates 170–176 on pages
98–99.
Cut out pieces and a strip of brown
felt measuring 39cm/15½in ×
14cm/5½in.

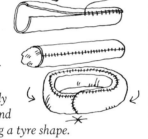

3 With small brown overstitches sew brown tail on opposite side of 'tyre' along straight edge.

• WHAT TO DO •

1 Fold strip of brown felt lengthways and overlap one edge 1cm/⅜in over the other. Taking care not to sew through to other side of strip, oversew together along this edge with brown thread. Keep ends open and stuff until softly rounded. Push one end into other end and oversew edge as before, forming a tyre shape.

2 Pin brown head pieces together and, using small neat overstitches in brown, sew around shape, leaving smaller curve open for stuffing. When softly rounded, attach to 'tyre' on either side of 'tyre' join (keeping long seam of 'tyre' below).

4 Add two red comb pieces on to head along seam with the same overstitching in red. Sew the two yellow beak pieces together with yellow overstitching and sew on to head just above bottom comb piece.

5 Cut two small circles of yellow felt and sew a black bead on to the centre of each with black thread. Glue into position.

6 Make a sandwich with the two black felt ovals and card – placing the card in the centre: glue the card to one piece and then glue the second felt piece on top. Finally glue around edge and press firmly on to bottom of tyre shape.

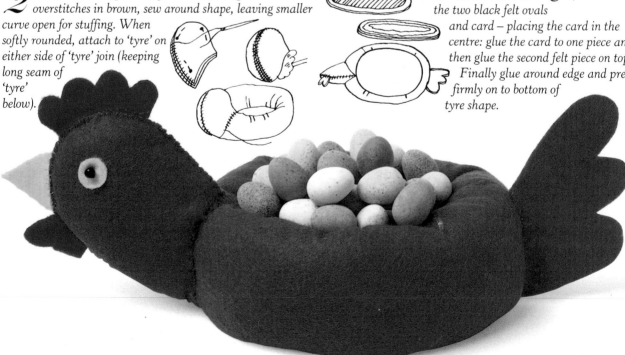

VALENTINE HEART

SHAPES TO CUT

See template 177 on page 99.
Cut out two heart shapes.

SHOPPING LIST

Felt:
2 × 20cm/8in squares of red
½ metre/½ yard of 1.5cm/⅝in
wide white lace
½ metre/½ yard of pink
sequins
Packet pearl-headed pins
Packet of coloured pearl-
headed pins
Packet of pins
Packet of steel-headed pins
Packet of silver bugle beads
7 small red sequins
14 large pink faceted sequins
7 large dark pink
faceted sequins
Packet of small pink sequins
1 fancy large red sequin
Packet of pearl beads
Packet of tiny red beads
Toy stuffing
Red and white thread

• WHAT TO DO •

1 Sew silver bugle beads on to one heart shape 3cm/1¼in from outside edge.

2 Sew felt hearts together with red overstitch, leaving small opening for stuffing. Stuff until very firm and solid. Sew up opening.

3 Turn over to back and sew lace below seam, making small pleats as you go with white stitches.

4 Turn over to front and carefully glue pink sequins (in strip) close to lace.

5 Now decorate with pins and beads and sequins – no sewing here. Divide bugle bead heart shape into two with row of coloured pearl-headed pins (push right in making sure none comes out through the back). Follow photograph, securing all sequins and beads with pins and completing one section at a time.

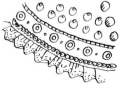

6 Finish with row of pearl-headed pins stuck through pink sequins alternating with steel-headed pins – in between bugle beads and glued strip of pink sequins.

CHRISTMAS STOCKINGS

SHOPPING LIST:
Reindeer Stocking
Felt:
25cm/10in of red
1 × 20cm/8in square of black

White 4-ply wool
Red and black thread

SHAPES TO CUT
See templates 178–180 on
pages 100–101.
Cut out the red stocking
pieces, red strips and
appliqué piece.

• WHAT TO DO •

1 With the toe
of a stocking
piece facing to
the left, pin the
reindeer in position
(facing left) at the top.
Sew with small neat
overstitching in black
thread.

2 Using the white wool and a
darning needle sew snowflakes
all over stocking around reindeer.

3 Pin the two stocking pieces together and sew
in red – either by machine with a zigzag
stitch or by hand with a running stitch if you prefer – leaving
the top open.

4 Sew the two red strips
together along each edge
either by machine or hand with a
running stitch. Fold in two and
push both ends 1.5cm/⅝in
into stocking top at right-
hand edge. Sew into position with
neat running stitches.

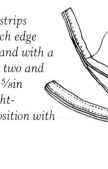

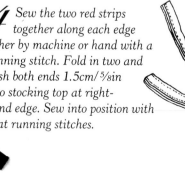

SHAPES TO CUT

See templates 178–184 on
page 101.
Cut out green stocking pieces,
green strips and appliqué
pieces.

SHOPPING LIST:

Christmas Tree Stocking
Felt:
22.5cm/9in of green
1 × 20cm/8in square of
dark green
1 × 20cm/8in square of
deep yellow
Scraps of white and red
Large red sequins
A few gold and red decorative
sequin shapes
Green, red, dark green, white
and yellow thread

• WHAT TO DO •

1 With the toe of a stocking piece facing left, pin
tree shape in position centred 7.5cm/3in from
top. Sew all round edge with small neat overstitching
in dark green.

2 Pin and overstitch tub with
red thread in position
centred under tree.

3 Sew white presents on
tree with white
overstitching and then sew a cross
on top with red thread used double
and a daisy stitching.

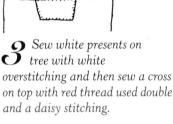

4 Sew stars on to tree and place one
on top with yellow overstitching.
Sew stars over stocking,
spacing them
evenly. Sew red
sequins and
decorative sequin
shapes in gaps
left on tree.

5 Pin the two stocking pieces
together and sew around edge in
green – either
by machine
with a
zigzag stitch
or by hand
with a
running stitch –
leaving the top open.

6 Sew the two green strips together
along each edge either by machine
or hand running stitch. Fold in two and
push both ends 1.5cm/⅝in into
stocking top at
right-hand edge. Sew
into position.

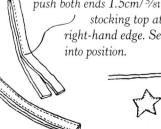

CHRISTMAS DECORATION

*Felt is a wonderful material for Christmas ornaments. The
bright, festive colours available mean that many attractive designs
can be worked. The following ideas may be hung on a
Christmas tree or incorporated into a table decoration.*

For star decoration
see page 64

For dove decoration
see page 67

For holly wreath see page 63

For teddy stocking
see page 66

For angel decoration
see page 65

HOLLY WREATH

SHAPES TO CUT

See templates 185–189 on page 102.
Cut out all the pieces.

SHOPPING LIST
Felt:
2 × 20cm/8in squares of dark green
1 × 20cm/8in square of green
Scrap of red
10cm/4in of red cord
20 small red wooden beads
Toy stuffing
Fabric glue
Green and red thread

3 Pin holly leaves, evenly spaced, around ring and glue down in position.

• WHAT TO DO •

1 Pin the two ring pieces together and overstitch in green around inner circle. Next sew around outer circle, leaving small opening for the stuffing.

2 Push stuffing in until rounded and firm. Put ends of cord (forming a loop) inside opening and secure when sewing up hole.

4 Sew red beads in between leaves around the inner and outer edges.

5 Make a bow by folding longer strip of red felt as shown and securing with stitch in red. Wrap shorter piece around stitched centre and sew together.

6 Sew bow at back on to wreath just below loop.

$\mathcal{S}$TAR $\mathcal{D}$ECORATION

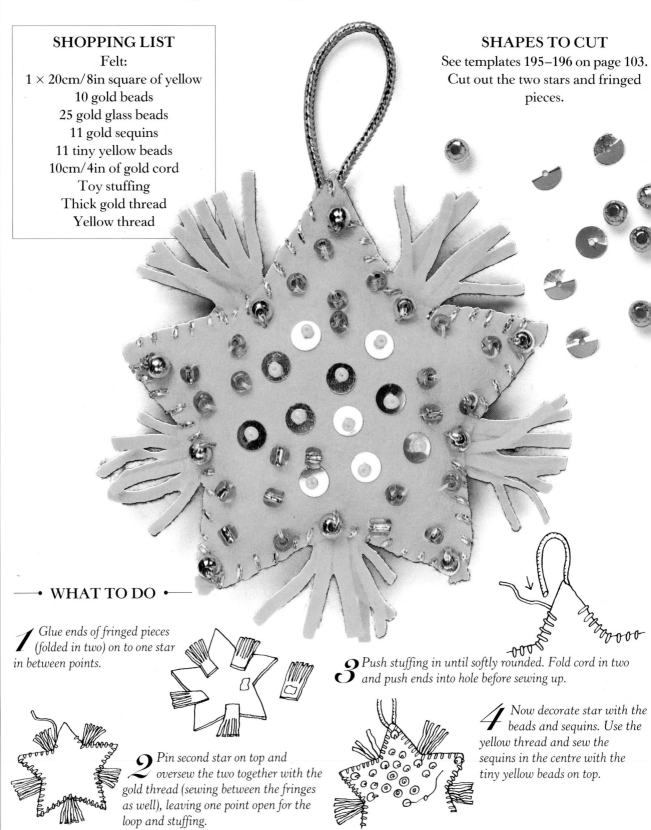

SHAPES TO CUT

See templates 195–196 on page 103.
Cut out the two stars and fringed
pieces.

WHAT TO DO

1 Glue ends of fringed pieces
(folded in two) on to one star
in between points.

2 Pin second star on top and
oversew the two together with the
gold thread (sewing between the fringes
as well), leaving one point open for the
loop and stuffing.

3 Push stuffing in until softly rounded. Fold cord in two
and push ends into hole before sewing up.

4 Now decorate star with the
beads and sequins. Use the
yellow thread and sew the
sequins in the centre with the
tiny yellow beads on top.

ANGEL DECORATION

SHAPES TO CUT

See templates 199–204 on page 103.
Cut out all the pieces.

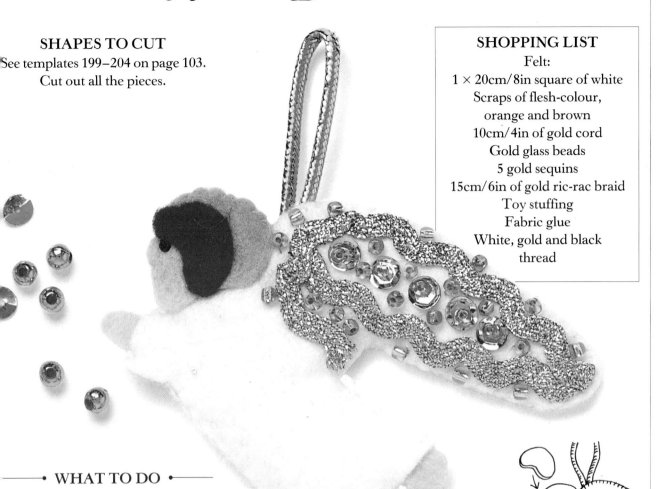

• WHAT TO DO •

1 Pin the two white angel halves together and sew together around edge with small neat overstitching in white. Start along the length of robe and when you reach the sleeve opening insert hand and sew in. Continue sewing around head, inserting ends of folded cord in between pieces at top of wing. When you reach the bottom of the robe, leave it open.

2 Push stuffing into shape until softly rounded. Push foot piece into top (angel facing left) of hole and sew up.

3 Glue face and halo in position and then the hair. Sew eyes with black stitching, making sure not to go through to the back.

4 Decorate the wing by sewing ric-rac braid in a loop around it.

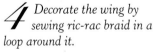

5 Add the beads and also the sequins with a bead sewn in the centre of them with gold thread.

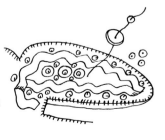

STOCKING DECORATION

SHOPPING LIST
Felt:
1 × 20cm/18in square of red
Scrap of mustard
Scrap of white
Scrap of green
5 small red beads
10cm/4in of red cord
Fabric glue
Toy stuffing
Black, red and
mustard thread

SHAPES TO CUT
See templates 190–193 on page 102.
Cut out all the pieces.

• WHAT TO DO •

1 Pin the two red stocking pieces together
and sew together all around edge (leaving
top open) with small neat red overstitching.

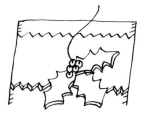

2 Glue white band
5mm/¼in down
from top.

3 Pin the three holly leaves on to band and
sew down, at the same time attaching
the five small beads in red thread.

4 Fold cord in two and sew
ends into top of stocking on
right-hand side, forming loop.

5 Now make the small teddy:
pin the two halves together
and sew all around edge in matching thread,
leaving top of head open for stuffing.
Push stuffing down into the arms and
legs and sew up opening.

6 Sew eyes, nose and mouth
with double black thread.
Push stuffing into toe of stocking
and a little way up, leaving enough
room for the teddy.

DOVE DECORATION

SHOPPING LIST

Felt:
1 × 20cm/8in square of white
1 × 20cm/8in square of grey
Scrap of yellow
12.5cm/5in of thin white satin ribbon
Transparent glass beads
Silver bugle beads
2 small black beads
2 pale blue sequins
Fabric glue
Toy stuffing
White thread

SHAPES TO CUT

See templates 194, 197–8 on page 103.
Cut out all the pieces.

• WHAT TO DO •

1 Pin the dove halves together and sew up with small overstitches in white, leaving a 2cm/¾in gap where the beak goes. Push the stuffing in here until firm and rounded.

2 Glue yellow beak pieces together and place just inside hole – then sew up with the dove halves.

3 Decorate the white wing pieces with three lines of bugle beads and a thick sprinkling of glass beads. Make sure the wings are facing opposite ways.

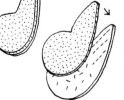

4 Glue grey wing pieces on to back of white wings. When dry, glue in place on either side of body.

5 Make eyes by sewing the black bead on to the blue sequins.

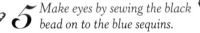

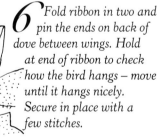

6 Fold ribbon in two and pin the ends on back of dove between wings. Hold at end of ribbon to check how the bird hangs – move until it hangs nicely. Secure in place with a few stitches.

*Copy a favourite image
to create your
own padded picture.*

*Using the Teddy template (from the Teddy
Nursery Frieze on page 32), cut two in any
colours and sew together to make a soft
toy. Add a stitched face and ribbon bow.*

VARIATIONS

Here are some variations which use the projects, templates and techniques in the book, but put them together in different ways or use different colours to create a completely new look. You can experiment and as you gain more experience in working with felt, you could use beads, decorative threads and bows to give your finished projects a new sparkle.

The Baby's Slippers (page 17) can be worked in white, blue or pink for a softer look. They will perhaps provide a special addition to a christening outfit.

The Bird Hat (page 14) – here in plain black felt with black stitching and the bunch of flowers pinned on the side.

Another simple idea for a needlecase.

Using self-adhesive felt, cover and decorate different-shaped boxes.

STITCHES AND TECHNIQUES

• STITCHES •

DAISY STITCH

Using the thread double, make a stitch and then bring the thread up from the underside in between the threads of the first stitch at the nearest end. Continue in this way making up a row.

BLANKET STITCH

This is used principally for securing and finishing double or more edges. Work from left to right. Having brought the thread up from the underside (at * on artwork), hold it down with your left thumb and insert the needle in a downward vertical position the required distance away. Pull it through the felt and the loop of thread – hold with thumb and continue with next stitch. When you are edging a largish item, use as long a piece of thread as possible to avoid too many joins.

An added decorative touch can be achieved by inserting a contrasting coloured thread under the blanket stitching (as in Mittens and Baby Slippers on pages 16-17).

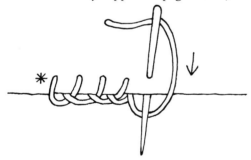

RUNNING STITCH

The length of the stitch and intervening spaces can be varied, but must be kept regular. Work from right to left.

To avoid wastage of your material, always place your stitching at the edge of the sheet of felt. Felt does not fray, so no seam allowance is necessary.

BACK STITCH

Work as for running stitch but when one row (or shape) has been finished, turn and work in the opposite direction filling in the spaces made by the first row.

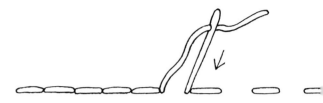

OVERSTITCH

Worked over a single or double edge either as a decoration or for strengthening purposes. Work from left to right.

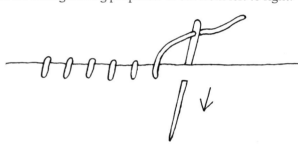

DECORATIVE STITCHING

The decorative stitches used in the projects are all straightforward and easy to work. Some tips on working these into attractive features are given below. A few stitches overlapping form a spot or an eye. When sewing a line such as a mouth use back stitch with a double spread. A shorter line such as a nose or teddy's mouth is made with single stitches touching one another.

A star can be made either by using single threads crossing each other in the centre of the stitch, or by using smaller stitches which end in the centre.

Mouth

Teddy's mouth

Bird leg and foot

Crossover star

The centres of simple flowers can be varied; either with or without a small contrasting felt spot in the centre, held down with decorative stitching.

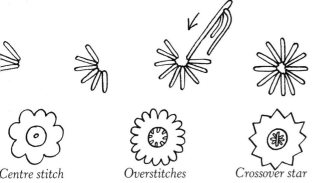

Centre stitch   *Overstitches*   *Crossover star*

FRENCH KNOT

The French knot is an attractive stitch, useful for creating a spot effect or for eyes.

Pull thread up from the underside of your fabric. Hold needle flat against felt and wind the base end of wool round the needle three or four times.

Hold the wound thread down in place with your left thumb and pull the needle and thread all the way through the fabric.

Push needle and thread back down to the underside, close to the knot.

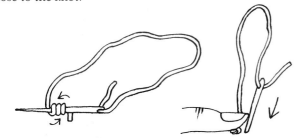

FINISHING OFF STITCHES

This technique is not needed when the piece you are working has an underside which will be covered up later. It is only important where the finishing will actually show on the completed item. This is particularly important in making clothes or gifts, where a 'professional' finish will enhance the quality of the work.

When you have finished sewing and want to cut off the remaining thread, the following technique is a neat, simple way to do it without leaving a lump.

Draw the thread (with the needle) under the appliqué piece or background felt and out at an edge. Cut off thread close to edge – there is no need to knot.

Appliqué piece

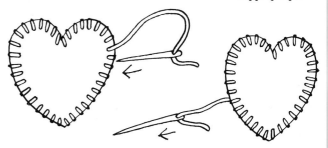

Stitching on background felt

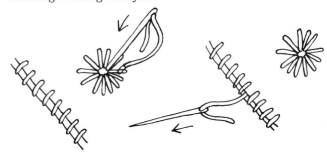

• TECHNIQUES •

USING THE TEMPLATES

Trace the template shape on to tracing paper. The templates in this book are always the correct size, except for the Waistcoat (on pages 18-19) and the Christmas Tree Stockings (on pages 60-61). These two templates should be taken to a photocopier and photocopied at 200 per cent (i.e. they are shown in the book at half their correct size). A small waistcoat could be made for the doll (pages 45-47).

Cut roughly around the shape and pin on to felt; to avoid wastage always place to the edge of the sheet of felt. Cut carefully just outside the line of the shape through the paper and felt. Unpin, and if more than one piece of the same shape is required, use the felt cut-out as your template from now on. Pin it on to felt and cut carefully, keeping close to cut-out.

Where a 'place on fold' instruction appears on a template, place this edge on to felt that has been folded in equal halves, along the folded edge.

In the case of an extended edging shape (as in the Teddy Nursery Frieze on pages 32-33) or a large number of the same shape, a card template can be made and drawn around on to the felt with a soft dark or light coloured crayon, depending on the colour of the felt.

Use a long pointed object to push the stuffing gently into the corners of an object, a little at a time. Continue stuffing until a firm, full but softish effect is achieved.

GLUING

Using a fabric glue, apply generously and evenly with the brush provided, spreading the glue on to one surface only.

Cover up to the edges, but avoid getting any glue on to front of the felt. Stick immediately and press firmly, smoothing over the surface. Leave to dry.

AFTERCARE
It is not advisable to wash felt as it can look matted afterwards. It can, however, be sponged clean or dry-cleaned (ask for advice at the dry-cleaners). Felt can safely be pressed. To remove specks of dust and hairs on the surface, simply dab over the felt with the sticky side of adhesive tape.

FRAMING PICTURES
Felt pictures are best left uncovered, backed onto card or plywood and framed. Cut the card to size (making sure you have enough background felt to fold over the edges) and simply tape securely round edges pulling gently, but firmly – first top and bottom and then the sides. Place in frame and hold in position with a backing.

APPLIQUÉ
As it is not necessary to turn in the edges of felt to neaten them, it is particularly suited for appliqué work. First pin or tack the cut-out in position on the background and sew down all the way around the edge with decorative stitches in thread or wool. Alternatively you can glue your cut-out pieces in position. You can also use padding under the cut-out pieces and part sewing, leaving some of the cut-out piece free from the background for a three-dimensional look.

POMPOMS
These can either be made from a single wool colour or a mixture.
1 Cut two circles out of thin card with a hole in the centre.

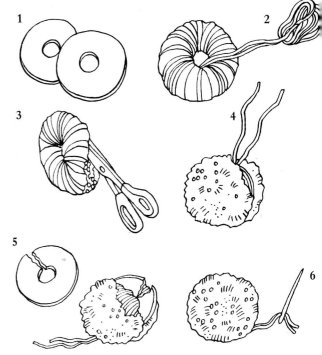

2 Keeping the two rings together, wind the wool evenly around them until the centre hole is full, changing the colour of wool every now and then if you want a multi-coloured effect.
3 Hold firmly in the centre and cut carefully through the wool around the outer edge.
4 Cut a piece of wool approximately 25 cm/10 in long and push carefully between the card rings, knotting the ends together tightly.
5 Cut the rings and remove.
6 Fluff up the wool and trim untidy ends leaving the long pieces to sew the pompom onto the felt item.

𝒯EMPLATES

*The following pages contain the templates you will need for all the projects
in this book. The numbers on the templates correspond to those referred
to on the project pages.*

*To make use of the templates you will need tracing paper, a pencil, sharp
scissors and pins. Trace the templates onto the tracing paper. Cut roughly
around each shape before securing it in position with pins on the felt. You
are now ready to cut the exact felt shape.*

*Apart from the templates for the Waistcoat and the Christmas Tree
Stocking, all templates are the correct size for use. The templates for
the Waistcoat and the Christmas Tree Stocking should be enlarged
by 200 per cent (that is, they should be used at twice the size shown in the
book). This can easily be done on a photocopier. Remember that the
template for the big slippers can be enlarged or reduced to fit the precise
size of foot required.*

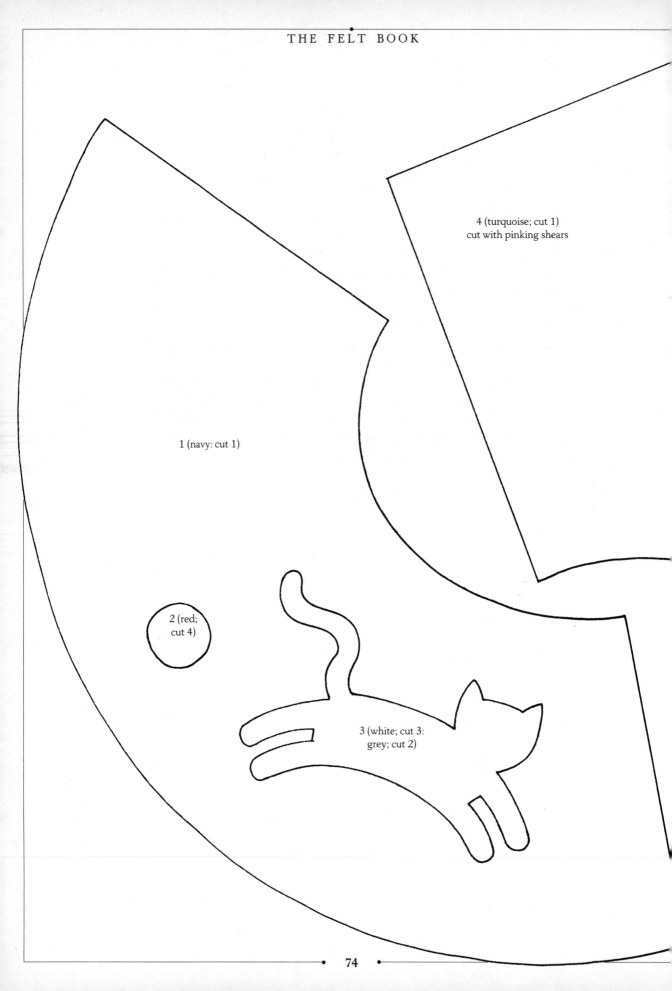

4 (turquoise; cut 1)
cut with pinking shears

1 (navy: cut 1)

2 (red;
cut 4)

3 (white; cut 3:
grey; cut 2)

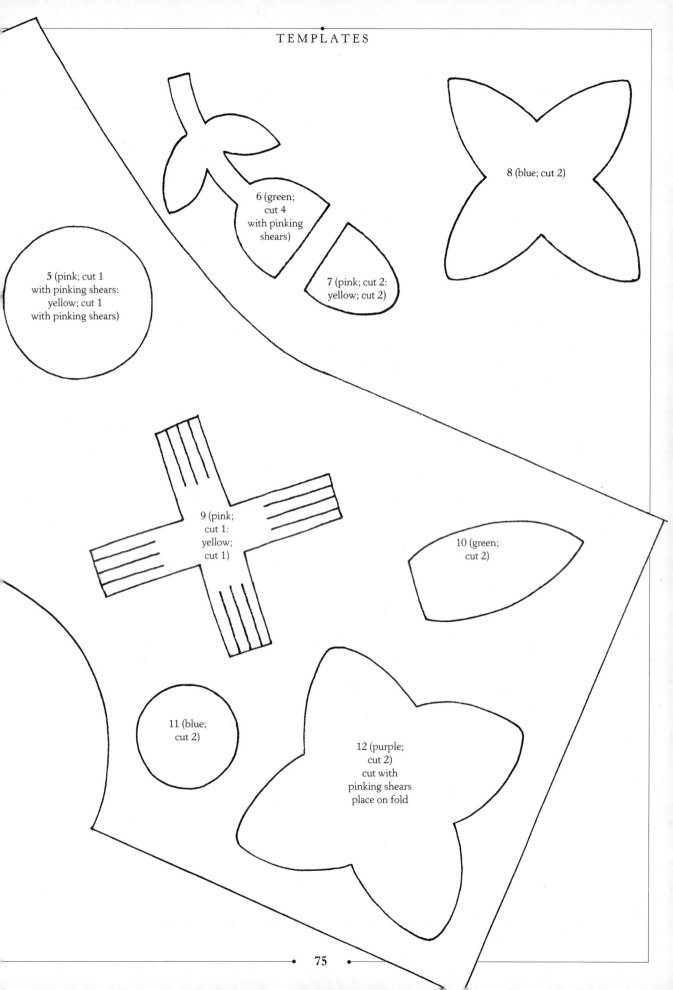

8 (blue; cut 2)

6 (green;
cut 4
with pinking
shears)

5 (pink; cut 1
with pinking shears:
yellow; cut 1
with pinking shears)

7 (pink; cut 2:
yellow; cut 2)

9 (pink;
cut 1:
yellow;
cut 1)

10 (green;
cut 2)

11 (blue;
cut 2)

12 (purple;
cut 2)
cut with
pinking shears
place on fold

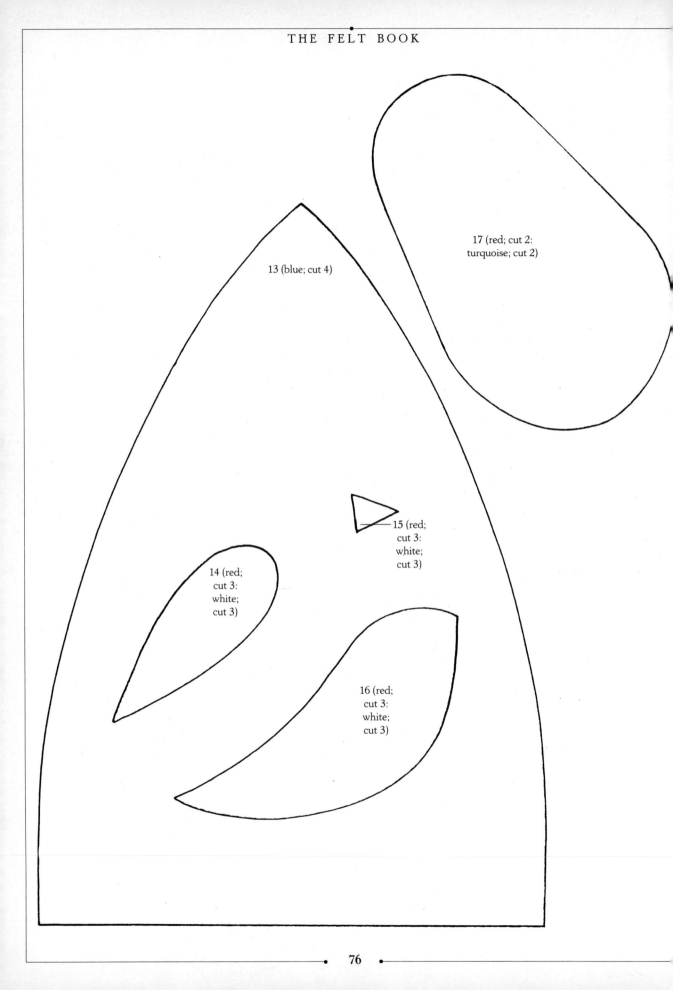

13 (blue; cut 4)

17 (red; cut 2:
turquoise; cut 2)

15 (red;
cut 3:
white;
cut 3)

14 (red;
cut 3:
white;
cut 3)

16 (red;
cut 3:
white;
cut 3)

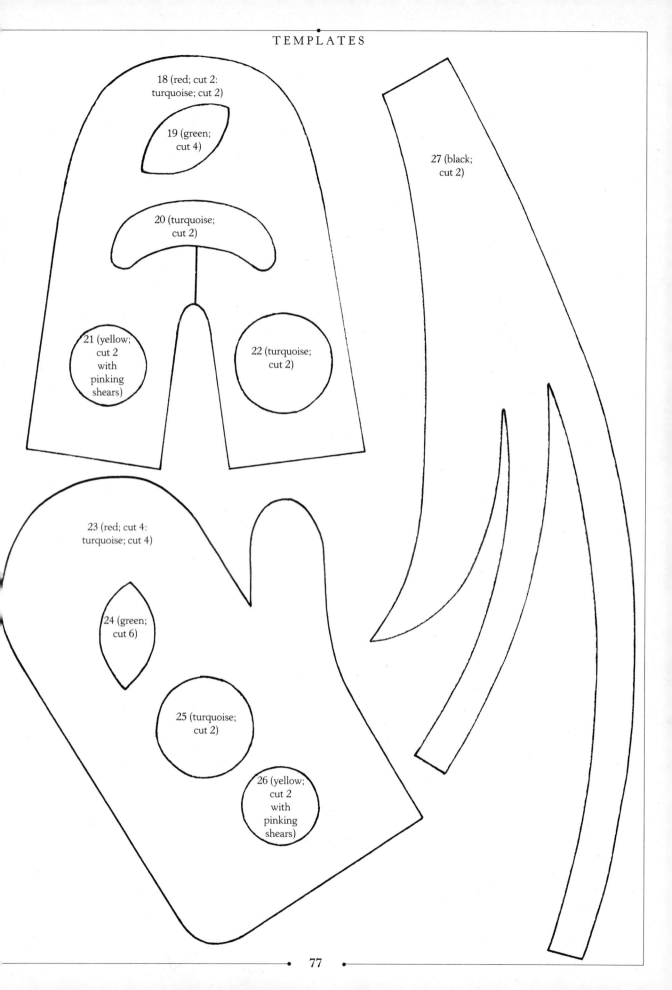

18 (red; cut 2:
turquoise; cut 2)

19 (green;
cut 4)

20 (turquoise;
cut 2)

21 (yellow;
cut 2
with
pinking
shears)

22 (turquoise;
cut 2)

27 (black;
cut 2)

23 (red; cut 4:
turquoise; cut 4)

24 (green;
cut 6)

25 (turquoise;
cut 2)

26 (yellow;
cut 2
with
pinking
shears)

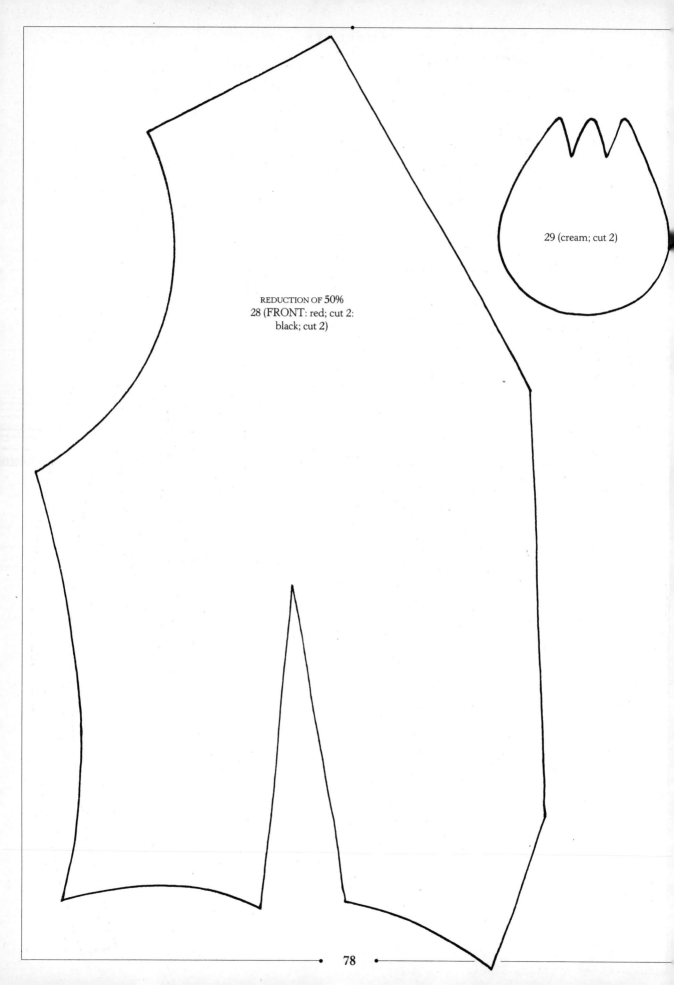

REDUCTION OF 50%
28 (FRONT: red; cut 2:
black; cut 2)

29 (cream; cut 2)

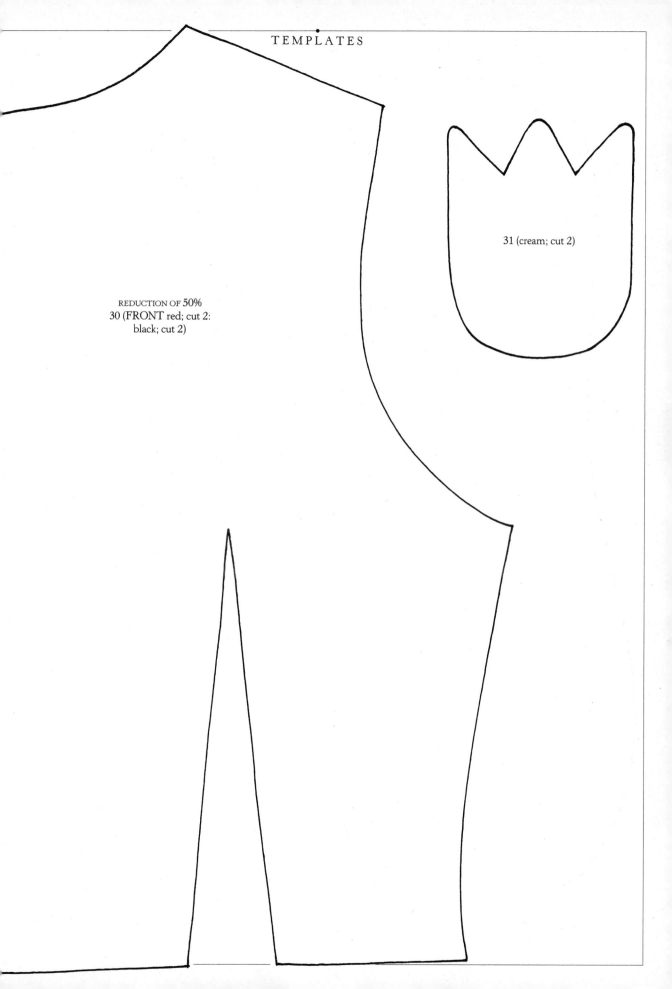

31 (cream; cut 2)

REDUCTION OF 50%
30 (FRONT red; cut 2:
black; cut 2)

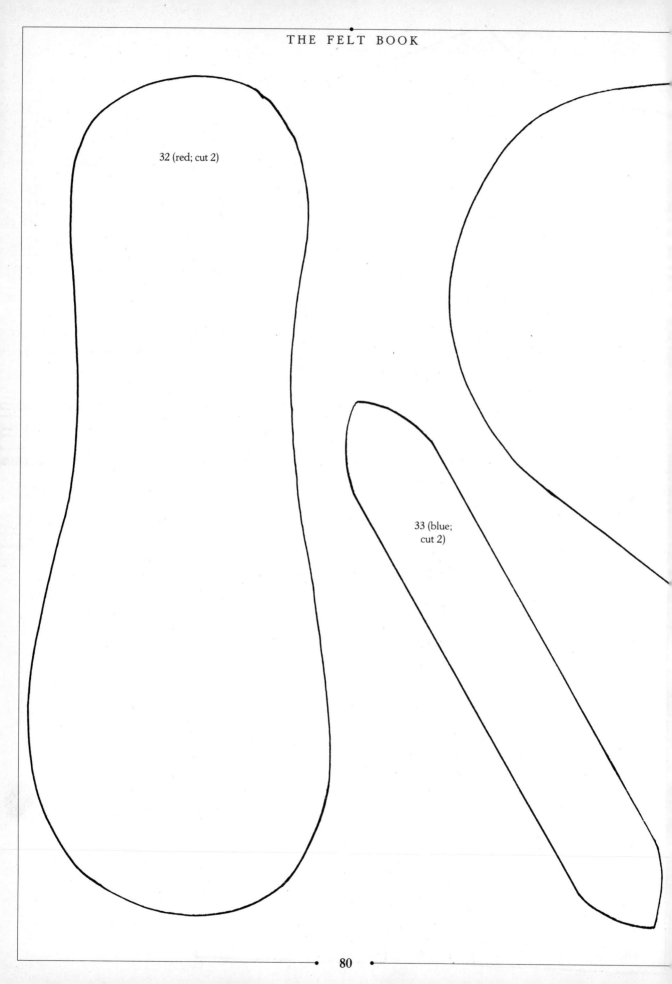

32 (red; cut 2)

33 (blue;
cut 2)

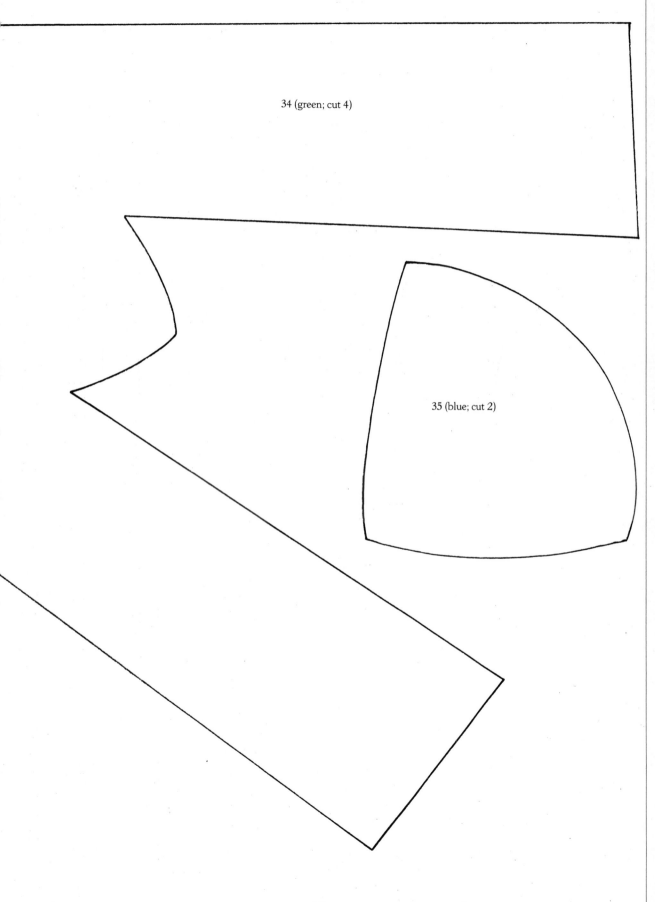

34 (green; cut 4)

35 (blue; cut 2)

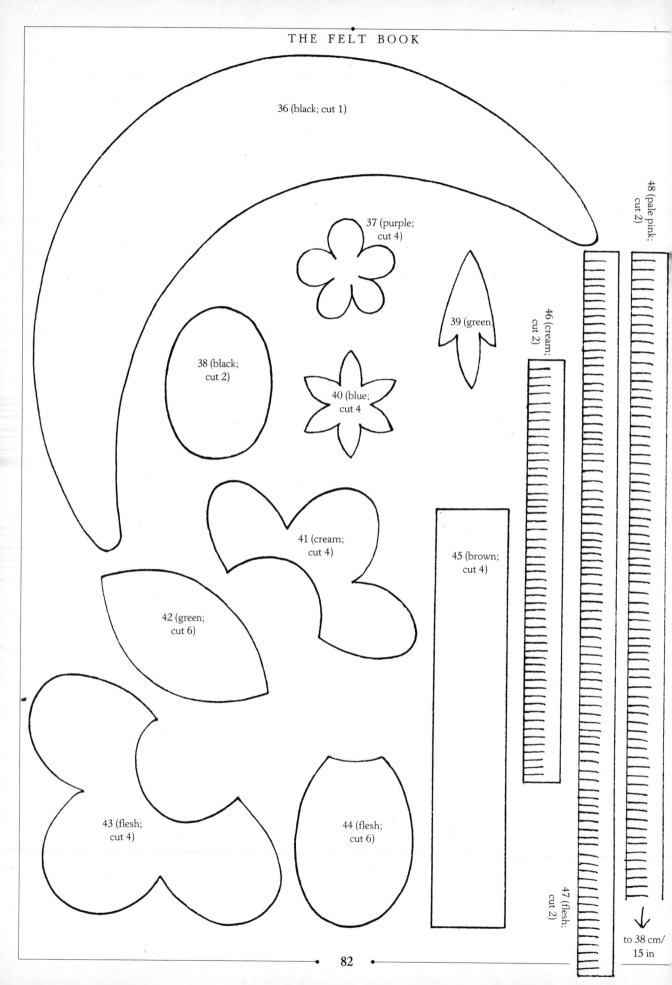

36 (black; cut 1)

37 (purple; cut 4)

39 (green

38 (black; cut 2)

40 (blue; cut 4

41 (cream; cut 4)

42 (green; cut 6)

45 (brown; cut 4)

46 (cream; cut 2)

48 (pale pink; cut 2)

47 (flesh; cut 2)

43 (flesh; cut 4)

44 (flesh; cut 6)

to 38 cm/ 15 in

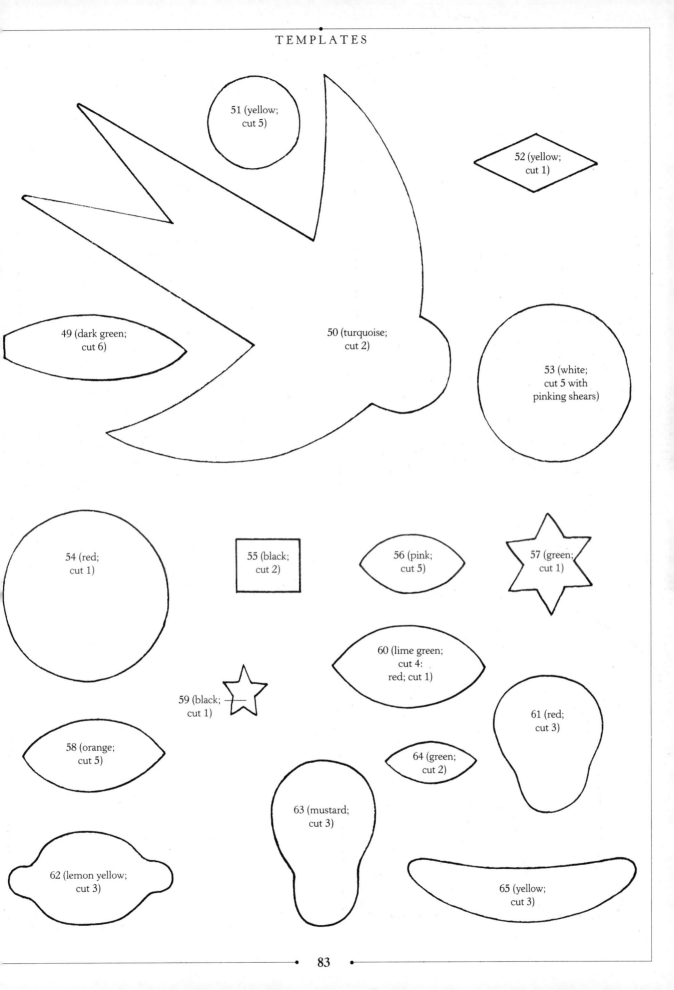

51 (yellow;
cut 5)

52 (yellow;
cut 1)

50 (turquoise;
cut 2)

49 (dark green;
cut 6)

53 (white;
cut 5 with
pinking shears)

54 (red;
cut 1)

55 (black;
cut 2)

56 (pink;
cut 5)

57 (green;
cut 1)

60 (lime green;
cut 4:
red; cut 1)

59 (black;
cut 1)

61 (red;
cut 3)

58 (orange;
cut 5)

64 (green;
cut 2)

63 (mustard;
cut 3)

62 (lemon yellow;
cut 3)

65 (yellow;
cut 3)

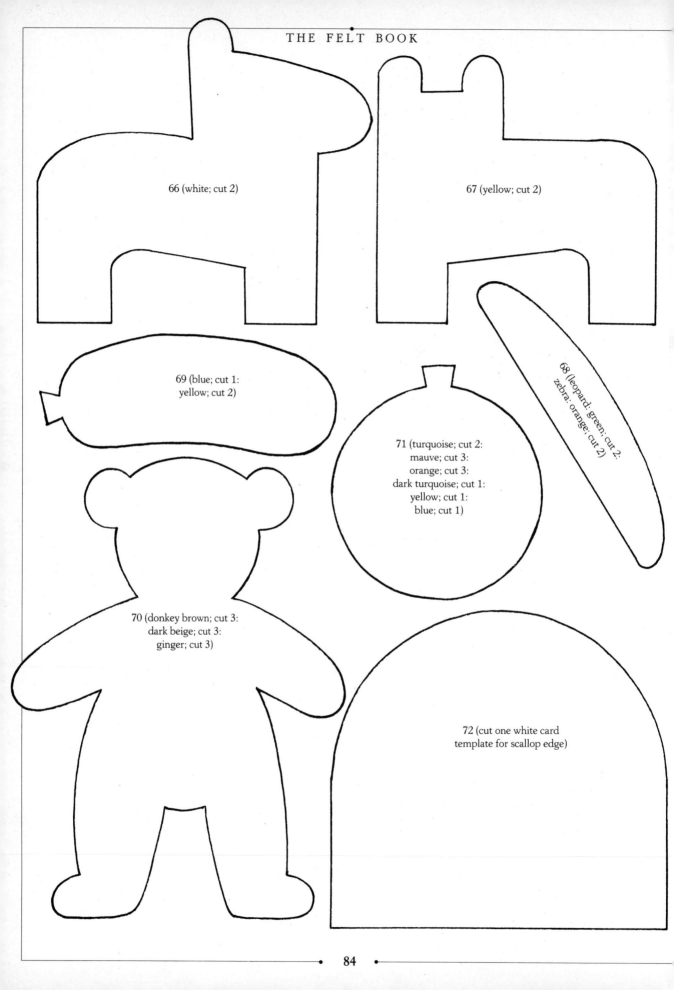

66 (white; cut 2)

67 (yellow; cut 2)

69 (blue; cut 1:
yellow; cut 2)

68 (leopard: green; cut 2:
zebra: orange; cut 2)

71 (turquoise; cut 2:
mauve; cut 3:
orange; cut 3:
dark turquoise; cut 1:
yellow; cut 1:
blue; cut 1)

70 (donkey brown; cut 3:
dark beige; cut 3:
ginger; cut 3)

72 (cut one white card
template for scallop edge)

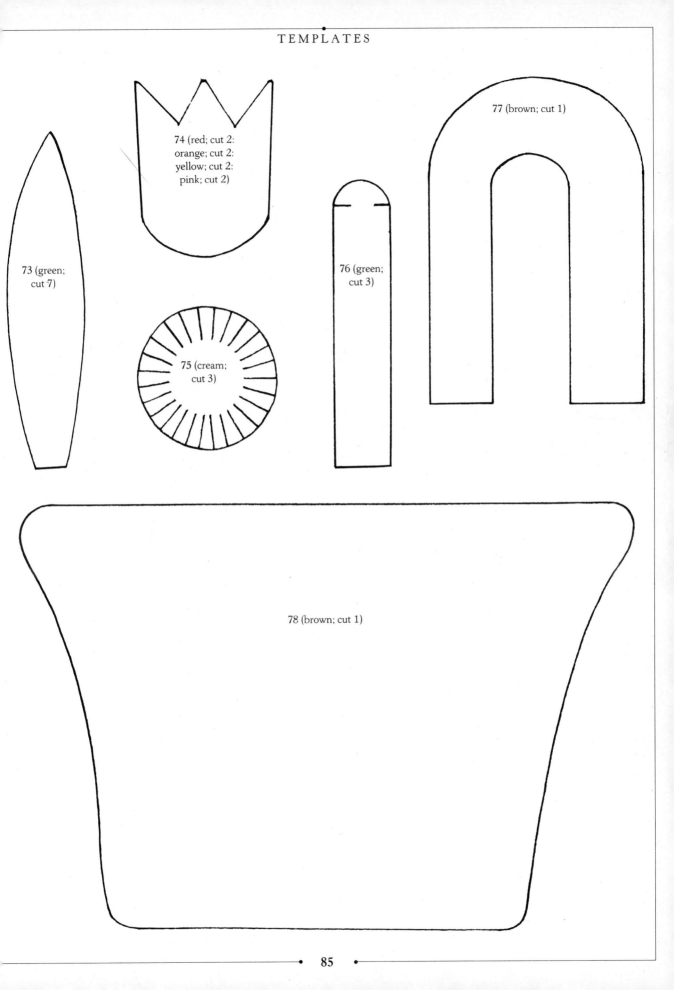

74 (red; cut 2:
orange; cut 2:
yellow; cut 2:
pink; cut 2)

77 (brown; cut 1)

73 (green;
cut 7)

76 (green;
cut 3)

75 (cream;
cut 3)

78 (brown; cut 1)

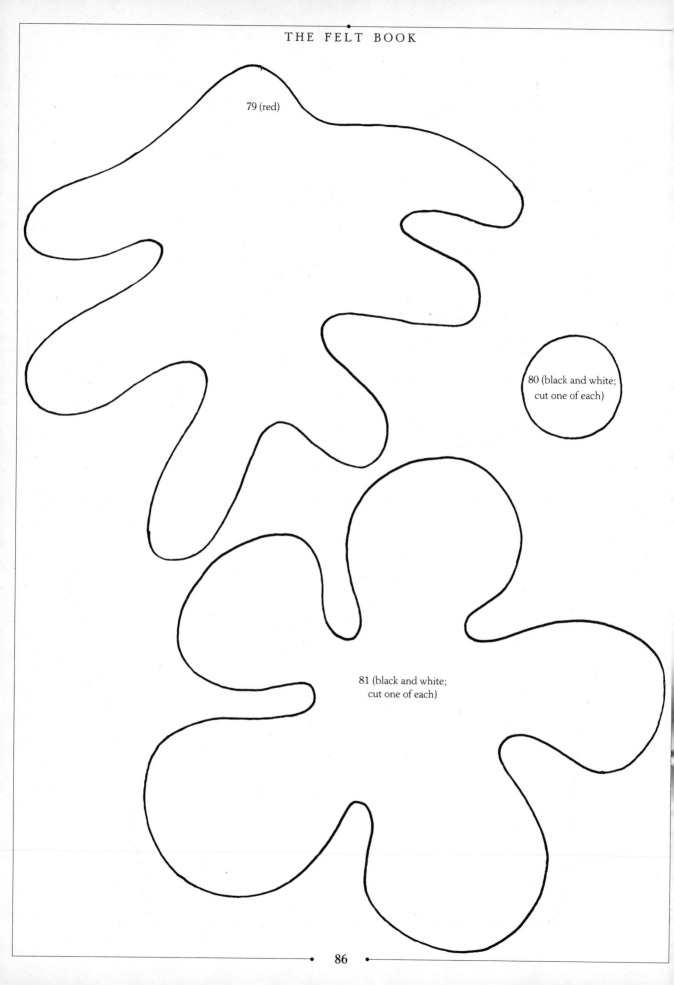

79 (red)

80 (black and white;
cut one of each)

81 (black and white;
cut one of each)

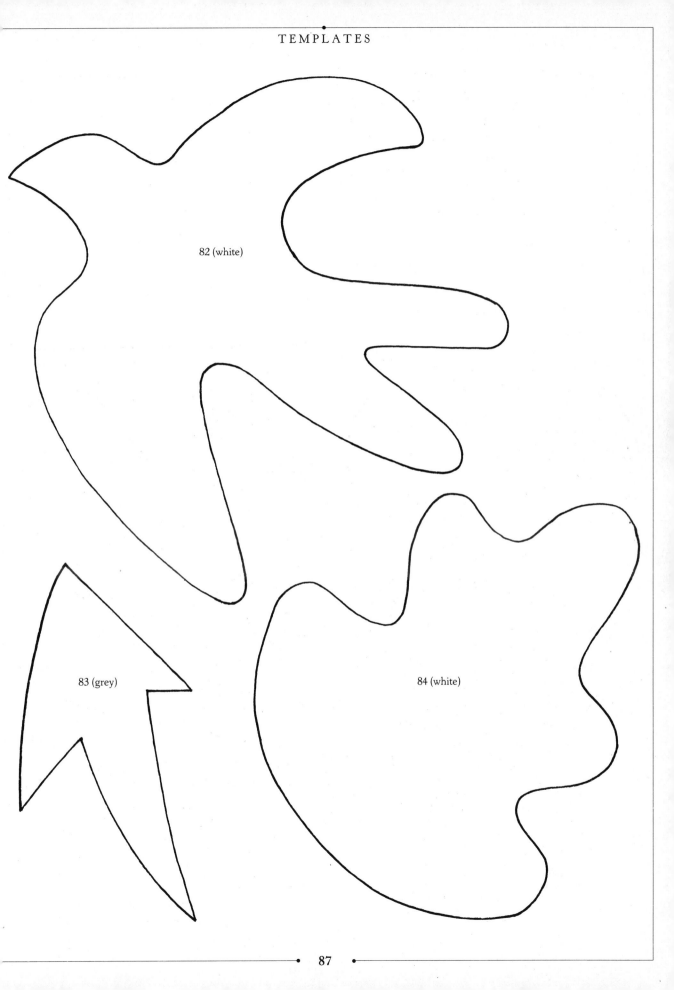

82 (white)

83 (grey)

84 (white)

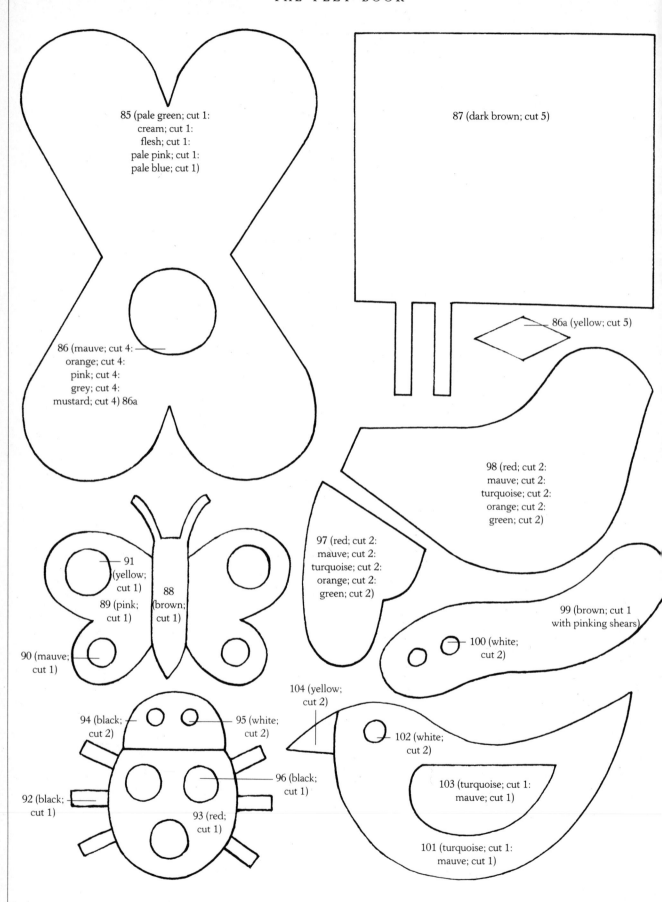

85 (pale green; cut 1:
cream; cut 1:
flesh; cut 1:
pale pink; cut 1:
pale blue; cut 1)

87 (dark brown; cut 5)

86a (yellow; cut 5)

86 (mauve; cut 4:
orange; cut 4:
pink; cut 4:
grey; cut 4:
mustard; cut 4) 86a

98 (red; cut 2:
mauve; cut 2:
turquoise; cut 2:
orange; cut 2:
green; cut 2)

97 (red; cut 2:
mauve; cut 2:
turquoise; cut 2:
orange; cut 2:
green; cut 2)

91
(yellow;
cut 1)

88
(brown;
cut 1)

89 (pink;
cut 1)

99 (brown; cut 1
with pinking shears)

90 (mauve;
cut 1)

100 (white;
cut 2)

104 (yellow;
cut 2)

94 (black;
cut 2)

95 (white;
cut 2)

102 (white;
cut 2)

96 (black;
cut 1)

92 (black;
cut 1)

103 (turquoise; cut 1:
mauve; cut 1)

93 (red;
cut 1)

101 (turquoise; cut 1:
mauve; cut 1)

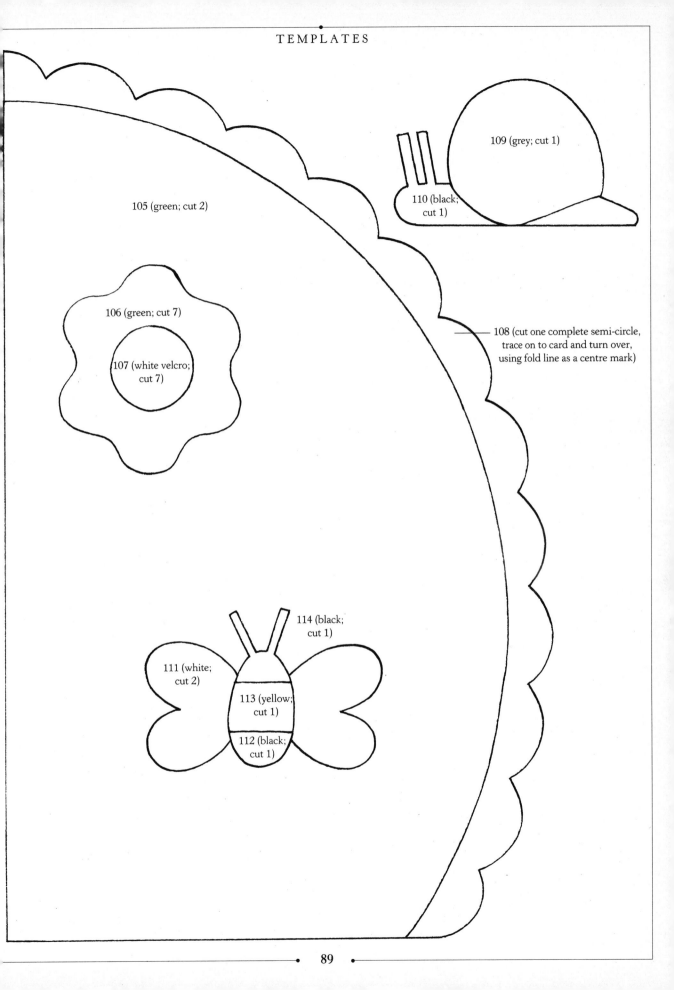

105 (green; cut 2)

106 (green; cut 7)

107 (white velcro; cut 7)

108 (cut one complete semi-circle, trace on to card and turn over, using fold line as a centre mark)

109 (grey; cut 1)

110 (black; cut 1)

111 (white; cut 2)

113 (yellow; cut 1)

112 (black; cut 1)

114 (black; cut 1)

115 (yellow;
cut 2)

116 (red; cut 2)

117 (yellow;
cut 12)

118 (yellow;
cut 4)

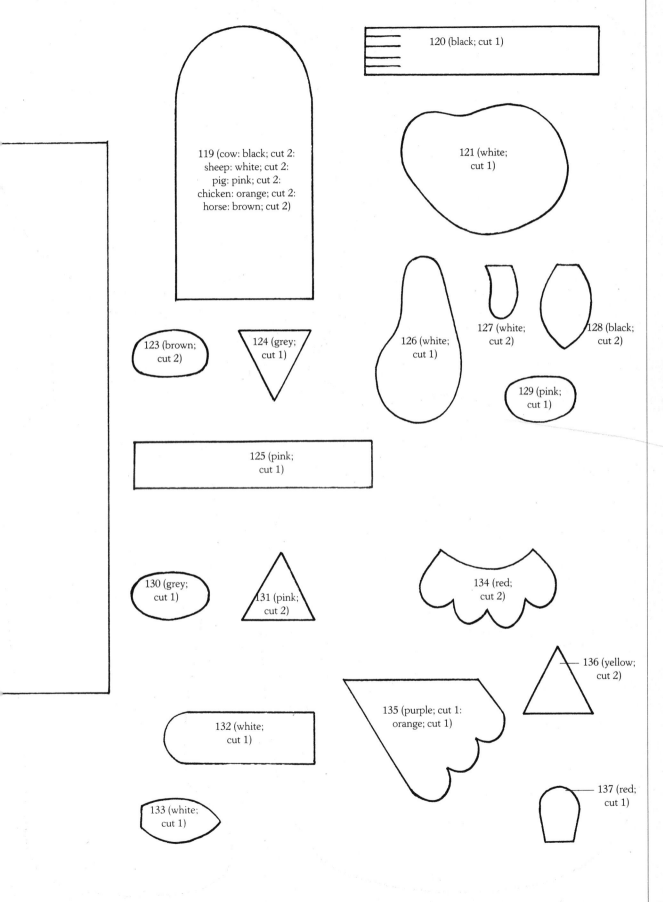

120 (black; cut 1)

119 (cow: black; cut 2:
sheep: white; cut 2:
pig: pink; cut 2:
chicken: orange; cut 2:
horse: brown; cut 2)

121 (white;
cut 1)

123 (brown;
cut 2)

124 (grey;
cut 1)

126 (white;
cut 1)

127 (white;
cut 2)

128 (black;
cut 2)

129 (pink;
cut 1)

125 (pink;
cut 1)

130 (grey;
cut 1)

131 (pink;
cut 2)

134 (red;
cut 2)

136 (yellow;
cut 2)

135 (purple; cut 1:
orange; cut 1)

132 (white;
cut 1)

137 (red;
cut 1)

133 (white;
cut 1)

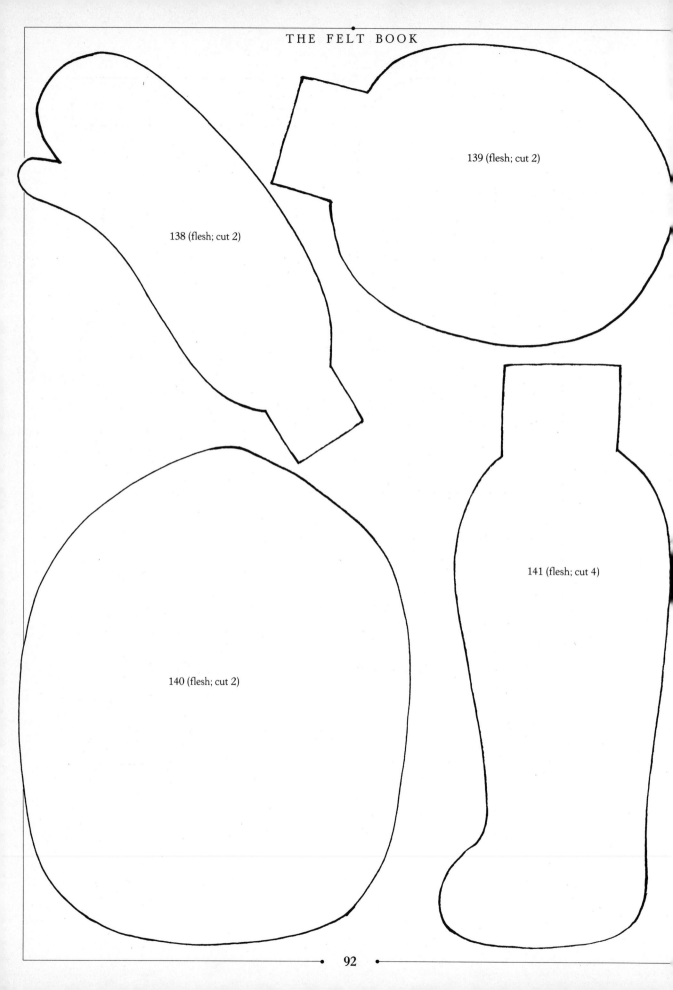

138 (flesh; cut 2)

139 (flesh; cut 2)

140 (flesh; cut 2)

141 (flesh; cut 4)

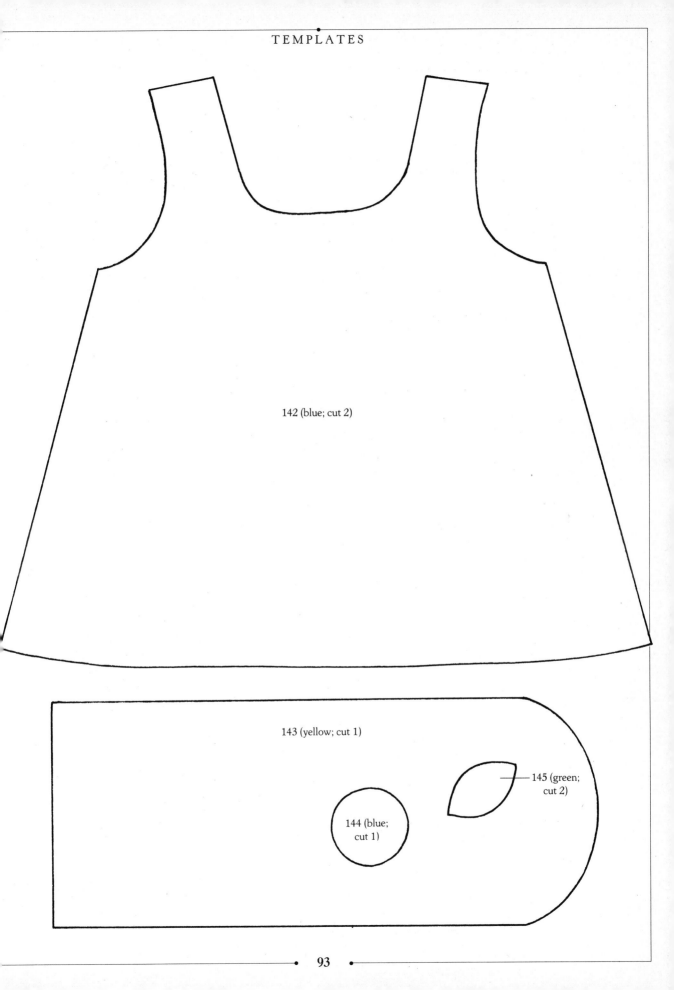

142 (blue; cut 2)

143 (yellow; cut 1)

145 (green;
cut 2)

144 (blue;
cut 1)

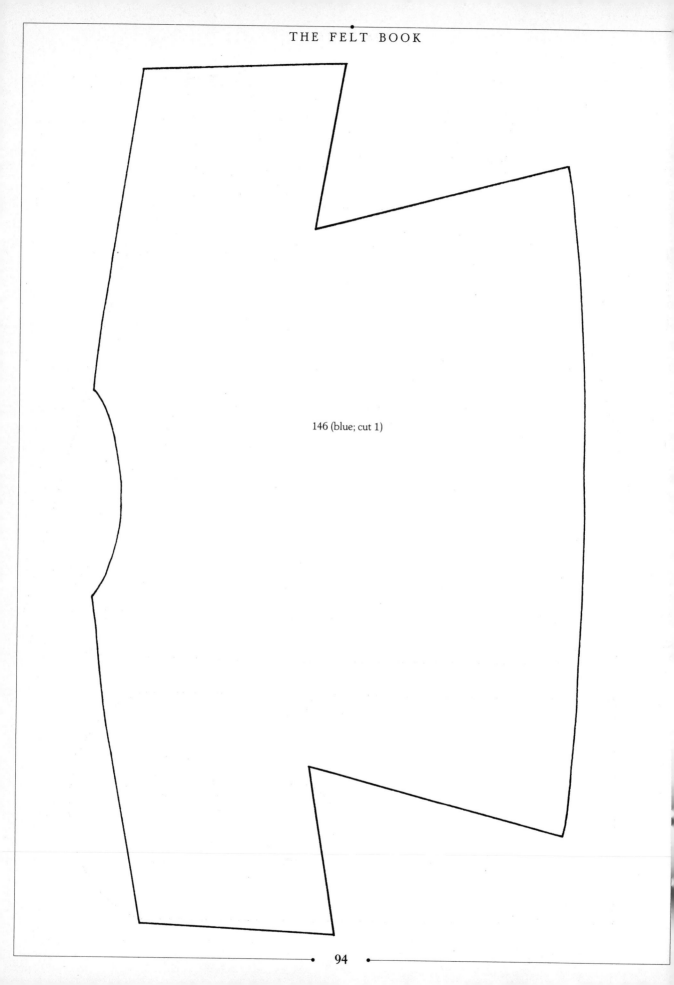

146 (blue; cut 1)

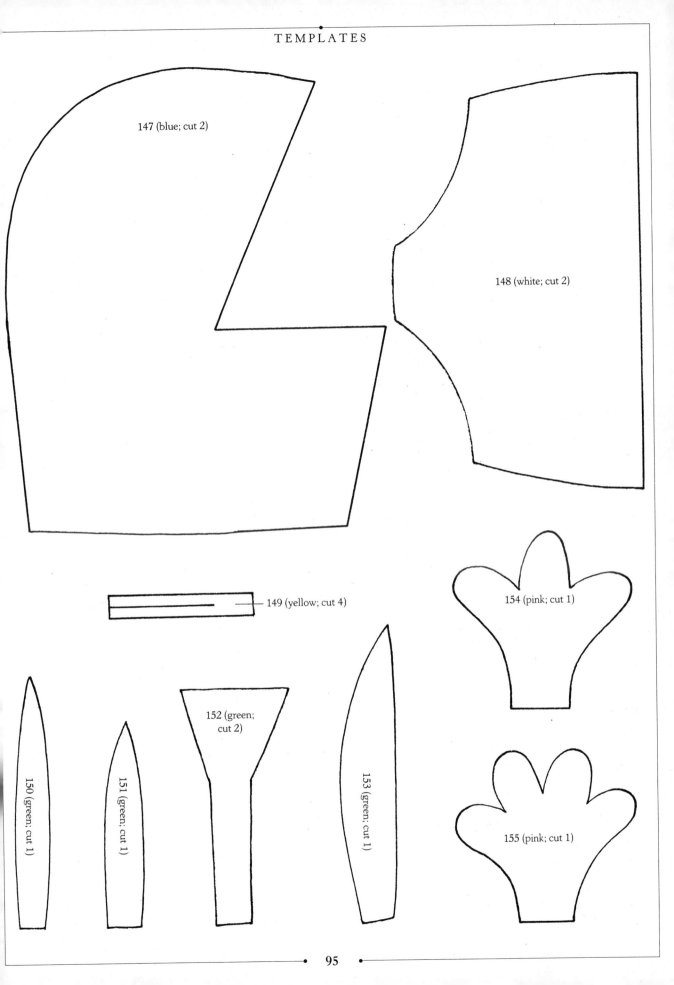

147 (blue; cut 2)

148 (white; cut 2)

149 (yellow; cut 4)

154 (pink; cut 1)

152 (green; cut 2)

150 (green; cut 1)

151 (green; cut 1)

153 (green; cut 1)

155 (pink; cut 1)

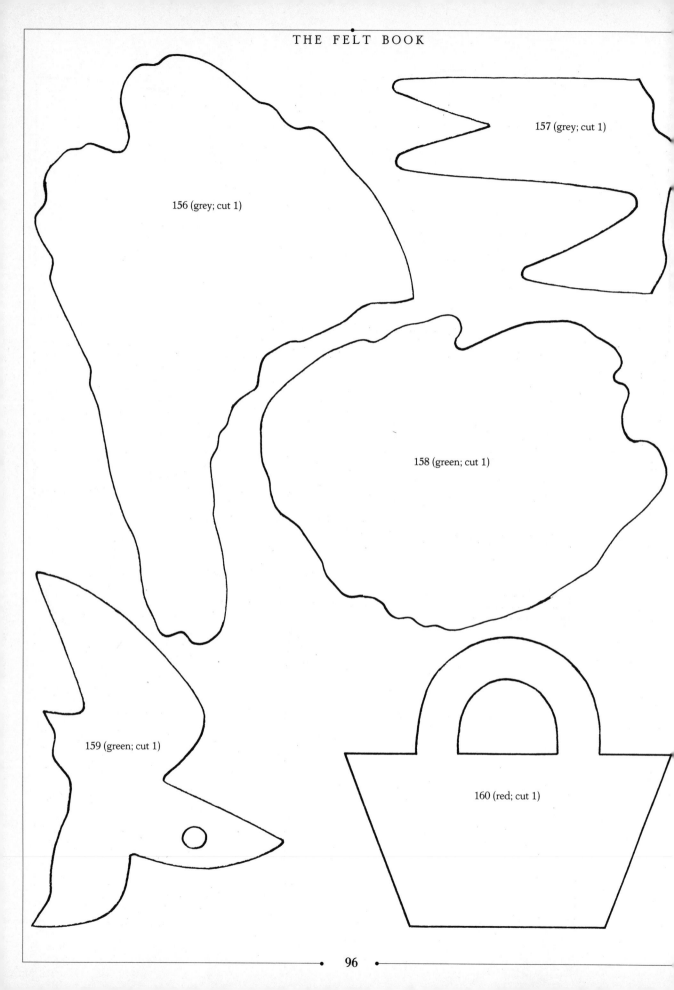

156 (grey; cut 1)

157 (grey; cut 1)

158 (green; cut 1)

159 (green; cut 1)

160 (red; cut 1)

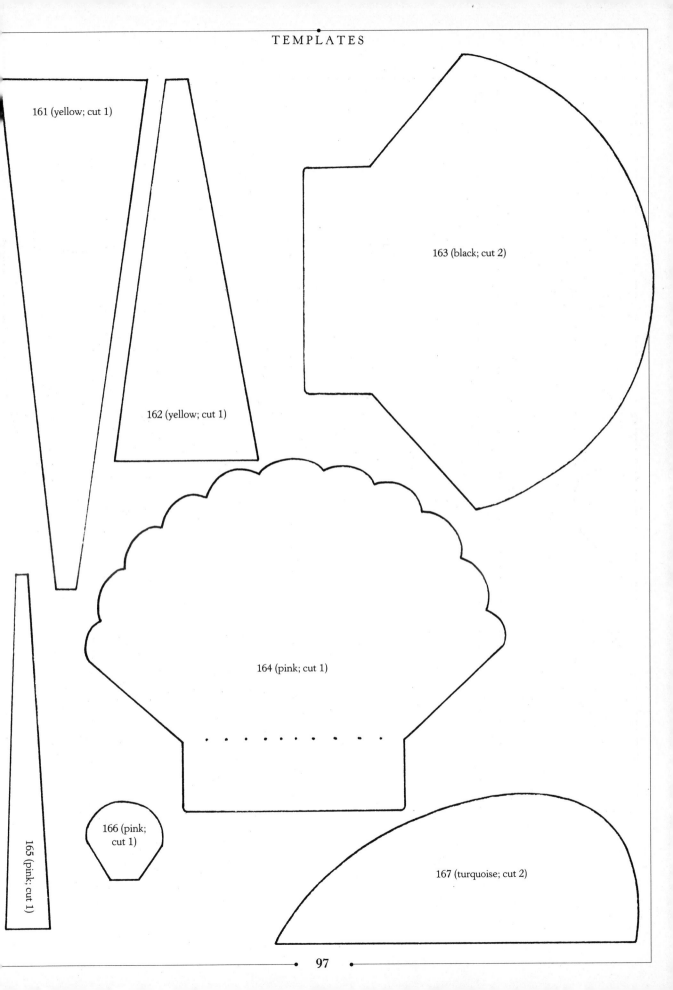

161 (yellow; cut 1)

162 (yellow; cut 1)

163 (black; cut 2)

164 (pink; cut 1)

165 (pink; cut 1)

166 (pink; cut 1)

167 (turquoise; cut 2)

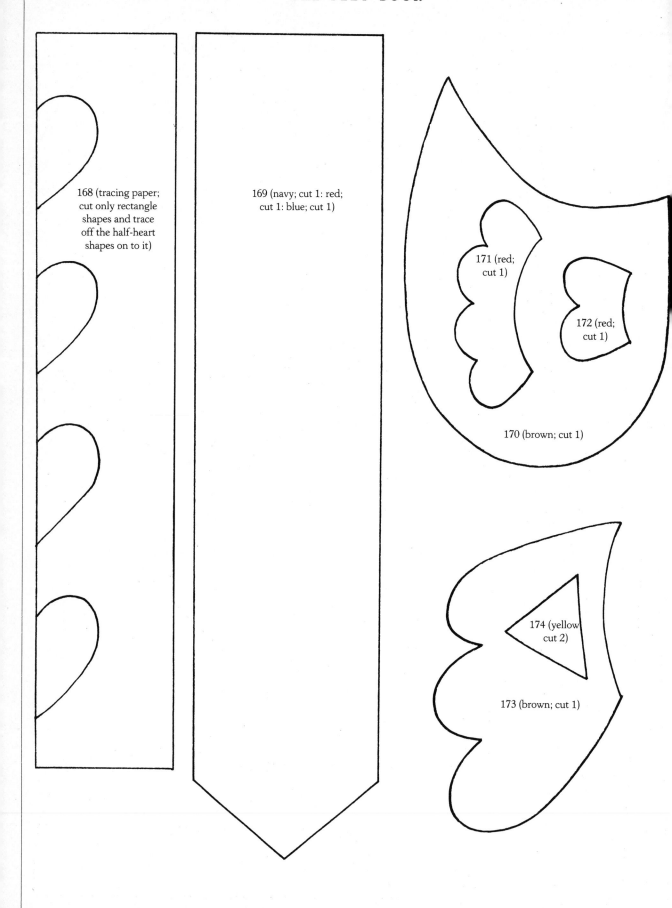

168 (tracing paper; cut only rectangle shapes and trace off the half-heart shapes on to it)

169 (navy; cut 1: red; cut 1: blue; cut 1)

171 (red; cut 1)

172 (red; cut 1)

170 (brown; cut 1)

174 (yellow cut 2)

173 (brown; cut 1)

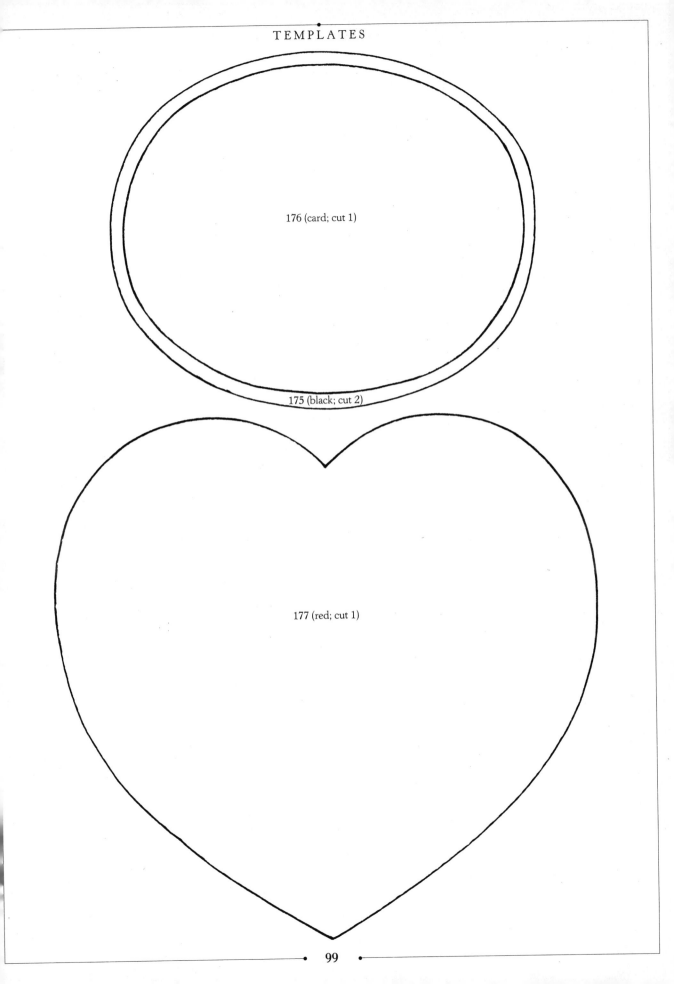

176 (card; cut 1)

175 (black; cut 2)

177 (red; cut 1)

REDUCTION OF 50%
178 (green; cut 2: red; cut 2)

179 (red; cut 2: green; cut 2)

181 (red; cut 1)

180 (black; cut 1)

182 (dark green; cut 1)

183 (white;
cut 3)

184 (yellow;
cut 15)

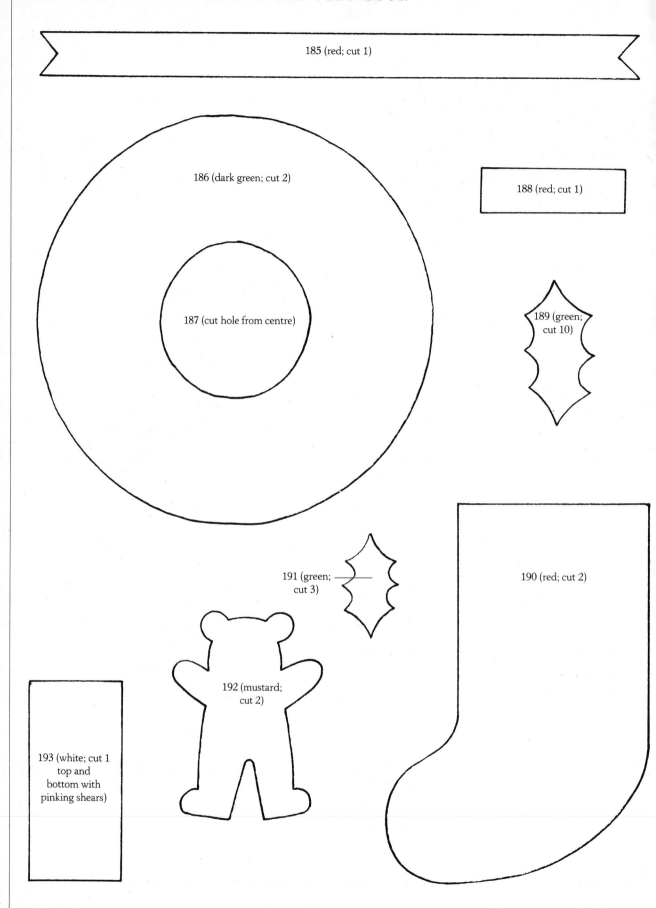

185 (red; cut 1)

186 (dark green; cut 2)

187 (cut hole from centre)

188 (red; cut 1)

189 (green; cut 10)

191 (green; cut 3)

190 (red; cut 2)

192 (mustard; cut 2)

193 (white; cut 1 top and bottom with pinking shears)

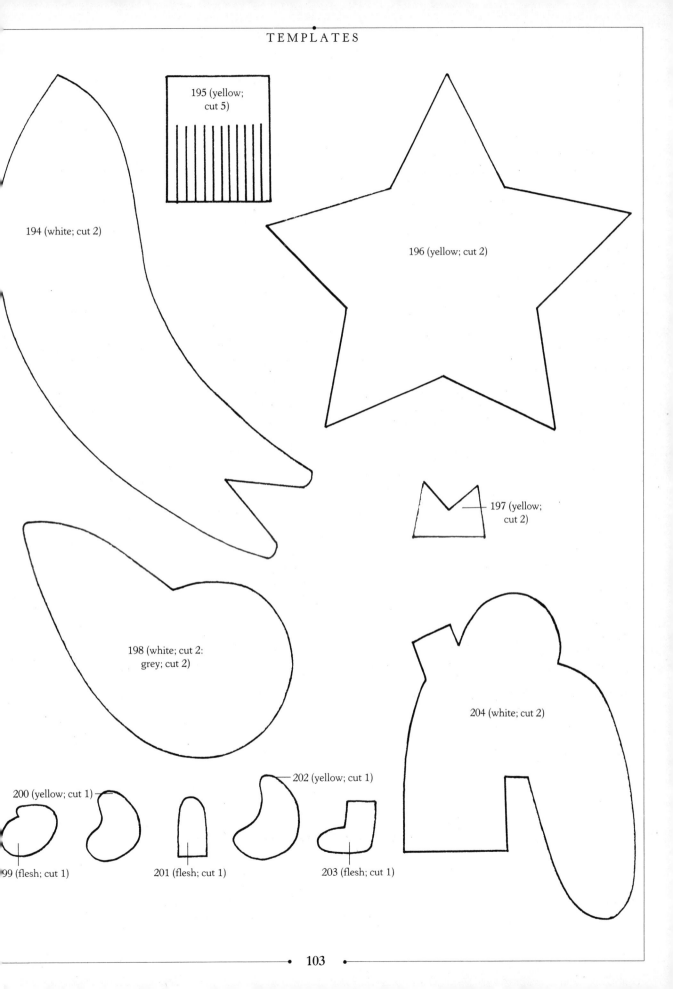

195 (yellow; cut 5)

194 (white; cut 2)

196 (yellow; cut 2)

197 (yellow; cut 2)

198 (white; cut 2: grey; cut 2)

204 (white; cut 2)

200 (yellow; cut 1)

202 (yellow; cut 1)

99 (flesh; cut 1)

201 (flesh; cut 1)

203 (flesh; cut 1)

ʃUPPLIERS

Felt is widely available. It can usually be found in craft shops, department stores and any shops which sell fabrics. Specialist shops, listed below, have the widest range of colours.

B. Brown shops stock over 60 colours and offer mail order for one metre (one yard) or more. Their retail shops are:

Zoffany House
74-78 Wood Lane End
Hemel Hempstead
Herts
HP2 4RF
Tel: 0442 68890
Fax: 0442 230896

Causeway House
Bath Street
Altrincham
Cheshire
WA14 2EJ
Tel: 061 929 8424
      061 928 4168
Fax: 061 926 9087

57-60 Clement Street
Birmingham
B1 2SW
Tel: 021 233 3514
      021 200 1333
Fax: 021 236 5178

78-89 Pentonville Road
London
N1 9LW
Tel: 071 696 0007
Fax: 071 404 0819

Marshall Street
Leeds
LS11 9AD
Tel: 0532 452192
      0532 456666
Fax: 0532 426389

Unity Street
Broad Plain
St Philips
Bristol
BS2 0HR
Tel: 0272 251875
      0272 293347
Fax: 0272 251729

105-107 Dumbarton Road
Glasgow
G11 6PW
Tel: 041 334 8284
Fax: 041 337 2642

J. W. Bollom shops stock over 80 colours. They do not do mail order. Minimum purchase is one metre (one yard).

1 Croydon Road
Beckenham
Kent
BR3 4BL
Tel: 081 658 2299
Fax: 081 658 8672

13 Theobalds Road
London
WC1X 8SN
Tel: 071 242 0313

314-316 Old Brompton Road
London
SW5
Tel: 071 370 3252

Unit 7, King William Enterprise Park
King William Street
Salford
M5 2UP
Tel: 061 876 4898
Fax: 061 876 5104

Unit 2, Windmill Industrial Estate
Birmingham Road (A45)
Allesley
Near Coventry
Tel: 0203 405151
Fax: 0203 404978

121 South Liberty Lane
Ashton Vale
Bristol
Tel: 0272 665151
Fax: 0272 667180

Unit 2, Thurston Granary
Thurston
Bury-St-Edmunds
Suffolk
Tel: 0359 32172
Fax: 0359 32306

Specialist Crafts Ltd. sell a wide range of colours both in different-sized squares and by the metre (yard). They also sell self-adhesive felt.

Retail outlets:
Specialist Crafts Ltd
Haramead Business Centre
Haramead Road
Leicester
LE1 2JW
Tel: 0533 510405
Mail Order:
Specialist Crafts Ltd.
P O Box 247
Leicester
LE1 9QS
Tel: 0533 510405

Fred Aldous is a craft shop with a wide range of colour sold by the metre (yard) and also many different-sized squares and shapes. Also bags of remnants and offcuts. It also has a mail order service.

Fred Aldous
37 Lever Street
Manchester
M60 1UX
Tel: 061 263 2477

Filze aller Art sells every imaginable colour, size and shape of felt, including thick felt (for such items as slipper soles). The shop in Munich Germany, has a mail order service.

Johanna Daimer
Filze aller Art
Dienerstrasse im Rathaus
8000 Munich 2
Germany
Tel: 01049 89 776984

----•ACKNOWLEDGEMENTS•----

I would like to thank Alan Beavon (Specialist Crafts Ltd.), Anni Pirchmoser (*Filze aller Art*), Geoff Naish (E.V. Naish Ltd.) and Stephen Winterburn (International Wool Secretariat) for their help. Also Jane and Sasha for lending me antique felt items which inspired the Bunch of Flowers and the Flower Necklace in this book. And last but not least my friends for their enthusiasm and encouragement.